A Change
of Heart:
Restoring Hope
In Marriage

Donald R. Harvey, Ph.D.

A Raven's Ridge Book

BAKER BOOK HOUSE
Grand Rapids, Michigan

Scripture references not otherwise identified are based on the King James Version of the Bible. Scripture references identified NIV are from the New International Version, Copyright ©1973 by New York International Bible Society. Used by permission.

ISBN: 0-8010-8911-5
Printed in the United States of America.

Dedication

"... there is nothing new under the sun."

—Solomon, Ecclesiastes 1:9 NIV

There is a sense that all of our *discoveries* are merely *rediscoveries*—yet they are discoveries which we need to make nonetheless.

This book is dedicated to Peter, Doug, Jan, Debbie ... all of my colleagues at CCS both past and present ... who as friends, more than colleagues, allowed me to bounce off my newly found insights and discoveries long enough for them to crystallize into books.

Contents

Introduction

The outline for *A Change of Heart* was penned on a Saturday afternoon in a Nashville hospital parking lot. I was sitting in my car waiting for Jan's return. Jan and I have always had a "social services" marriage. My role has been therapist while Jan's has been social worker. At that particular time, Jan was employed by a Christian agency with a ministry to women with unplanned pregnancies. One of the girls Jan had been working with had delivered her baby. The girl had chosen to place her child for adoption. Jan was at the hospital to give emotional support and to take responsibility for the newborn infant. A childless Christian couple eagerly awaited the opportunity to love and raise this child.

As I sat in the car, my thoughts kept gravitating back to the act of *redemption*. Most importantly, there is redemption in its spiritual sense—God's plan for the salvation of mankind. But God's redemption plays a larger role in the activities of mankind than solely in the spiritual realm. I marveled at how God could come into a situation as problematic as the unplanned birth of this child—one encumbered with a myriad of complex emotions and involving many lives—and bring order out of chaos. He brought peace where there was anxiety; healing where there was pain; and hope where there was only apprehension. In short, He brought redemption.

As precarious a start in life as this may have been for this newborn infant, all things appeared to be "working together for the good." In spite of the undesirable consequence of an impulsive act that occurred several months earlier, people were allowing the Father to redeem the situation.

After marveling at the redemptive nature of God being displayed in this situation, my thoughts reflected back upon the week I had just experienced. It had been a difficult and perplexing week for me. I had begun counseling with four new couples during the days leading up to the weekend. That was not unusual. What was unusual, however, was the similarity in their presentations. The cosmetic features were different enough. Each couple presented a different situation—they possessed different personalities and there had been different events in their marital histories. But though the particular idiosyncrasies which made up their stories were different, the same theme was present in each marriage. In each marriage one of the partners had lost hope. Their emotional hearts were failing. And with the loss of hope came a marital crisis. It is what they shared in common—the loss of hope—that I have addressed in this book.

The focus of *A Change of Heart* is on redemption—redemption of marriages in crisis. In it I chronicle how hope is lost. **More importantly, I share how hope is regained.** Hope can return. Relationships can be different. Hearts can be changed. God has a plan. But we must be willing to do our part if He is to be allowed to do His.

Though I address specifically the situation of marriages that have lost hope, I believe there is no situation so desperate as to be beyond the healing and restorative power of God. There is nothing irredeemable. Whether it be situations like unplanned pregnancies which are frequently the result of a single act; or marital crises which are usually the result of more repetitive behaviors; God is able to bring redemption. We need only to let Him.

Don Harvey
Nashville

I

The Loss of Hope

1

Terri's Story

Jan and I have lived in many different places over the course of twenty years of marriage. When it came to pursuing graduate degrees and a professional career, it seems that moving from one place to another just naturally went with the territory. Although leaving one area for another has never been easy, one of the benefits has been the number of friendships we have established across the country.

We have now abandoned our nomadic lifestyle and settled in Nashville, Tennessee. Nashville is a tourist area with plenty to see and do. It is not only a fun place in its own right, but also conveniently lies along the pathway to other popular destinations. All in all, it has proven to be a great place to live if you want to periodically renew old acquaintances. And we do. Our guest bedroom is ever ready, as are additional trundle beds. And on many occasions, we have had the opportunity to house other families, reminisce about the good old days, and catch up with what's new in each other's life.

Another reminiscent weekend—that's what was supposed to happen. Terri and her three daughters would be arriving Friday night. Robert had to be out of town on business and could not make the trip. But Terri wanted to come anyway. If events followed traditional visitor scripts, we would find ourselves well past midnight hard at the task of catching up and renewing old friendships. After a hearty breakfast the next morning, Saturday would involve a full day of activities. There would be some sight-seeing, shopping, and possibly a visit to Opryland, our local amusement park. We would all be physically drained by the end of the day, but the time spent together would have made it well worth the effort. Sunday would bring a welcomed change of pace. Our two families would attend church services, followed by a final meal together. After a brief rest and a hurried packing of a waiting car, we would say good-bye to our friends. With renewed memories, we would once again look forward to a future reunion.

That's what was supposed to happen. Just another reminiscent weekend. Then I got a phone call from Robert which changed the complexion entirely. With the normal salutations dispensed, Robert immediately proceeded to the purpose of his call.

> Don, you're talking to a desperate man. Terri has told me that she plans to visit you and Jan this weekend. I want you to know that the entire future of my marriage may rest on what happens while she's there. She's planning to divorce me. Please talk to her. Convince her to stay. I don't want my marriage to end.

Robert's voice matched his self-reported description: desperate. There was intensity and quickness in his words. This was far different from the Robert I had known over the years. I was used to a man who had few serious comments. Relating had always been easy and light-hearted.

You know how it works with couple relationships. Often all four individuals are strongly invested into the friendship. However, Robert and Terri represented one of those relationships where the wives were fairly close but the husbands were not. Jan and Terri were close. But Robert and I were little more than acquaintances. He had always tended to keep our personal conversations on a safe, superficial level. I really didn't know him very well.

> We've been having some problems for the past few years. Well, really, we've had problems on and off over most of the marriage. But things have never been this bad.

I was aware that there had been problems. Some of these occurred before we met Robert and Terri. Their relationship was still developing problems since the four of us became friends. Terri had spoken to Jan about their marriage when we lived in the same community. And after we moved away, Terri had once sought my advice by telephone during a time when she and Robert were briefly separated. But this was the first indication of any kind from Robert that the marriage had seen rough times. He had always been more protective of his image, careful to project that everything was fine.

> I've done some things that I'm not very proud of. Some things that I wish I could undo. But I can't.
>
> Terri has been really hurt by it all. Sometimes I've said things intentionally meant to hurt her. There has even been another woman. That ended quite a while ago, but I don't think Terri has gotten over it.

Robert did not offer many details of his personal indiscretions. The brief allusion to an affair was as specific as he got. The specifics were obviously something which he didn't wish to discuss or dwell upon. Knowing Robert, it was probably difficult enough for him to even admit anything was his fault—anything he would have to take some responsibility for.

Unknown to Robert, I was already aware of more than he would be comfortable that I knew. I don't like being in the position of a secret bearer, but Terri had shared much of their marital history when she sought my professional advice during their separation. Reportedly, some of what Robert "was not proud of" could include a nature that was both rigidly controlling and selfishly insensitive. Things had to be his way, and nobody's needs were as important as his. If Robert didn't want Terri to do something, she had better not do it. Otherwise, she was challenging his authority and then subject to his wrath.

Tension points throughout the marriage had been her friendships, work, and education (Terri had returned to college). Robert was opposed to any of these for Terri. Anything that had the potential of pulling Terri away from a total dependency upon and subserviency to him was viewed as threatening and was to be resisted. Terri's continued pursuit of any of these areas, therefore, meant that she had to incur Robert's retribution.

Robert wanted control. According to Terri, he was willing to go to great lengths in order to both gain and keep it. His primary mechanism for accomplishing this was force. Sometimes his force was physical. Robert had never struck Terri, but he had pushed and shoved her. And when very angry, there had been the threat of worse. At other times, his coercion was through manipulation. He controlled the finances so Terri could not spend any money without his consent. This made going to college, with its tuition costs, very difficult.

Probably nothing was more powerful than Robert's verbal barrage. Constantly, he was demeaning. If you believed Robert's words, Terri wasn't "good enough" as a mother, wife, or Christian. She wasn't "smart enough" to make it in either college or the business world. And she wasn't "pretty enough." Robert was generous in his comments about the attractiveness of others, but sparing when it came to Terri. And when needing to keep her under control, he only had disdain for her appearance, ever ready to point out Terri's physical imperfections.

Desperately clinging to a battered self-esteem, Terri languished in a gulf that separated two extremes. At one end of the continuum was total surrender of self to the control of another while at the other was emotional balance and personal autonomy. **The latter is not contradictory to a healthy marriage. In fact, it is a prerequisite.** But Terri's persistence for emotional health, as though clinging to life itself, brought only increased pressure from Robert. He was determined to be in control.

So, I was aware that there had been problems—aware that everything was not as it had appeared—aware that all was not fine—and aware that Robert had legitimate reasons for which to feel regret.

> I've never seen Terri like this before. She won't even talk to me about it. You're my last chance.
>
> You can tell Terri I called if you think it'll help. Do what you think is best. All I know is I don't want my marriage to end. I pray it's not too late.

What was to be a light-hearted and fun-filled time with an old friend suddenly took on a heaviness. Responsibility is that way. I did not feel as though it were my responsibility necessarily to talk Terri into or out of anything. After all, she was an adult. But Terri and Robert were my friends. They were people I cared about. It did seem appropriate to talk with Terri about her marriage and to help her sort things out. This was likely to be a topic which Terri had little desire to discuss—and one that would undoubtedly be sensitive.

Terri and her children arrived as planned and the events of the weekend followed the anticipated format. We talked late into Friday night, were tourists on Saturday, and worshiped on Sunday morning. Terri shared what had been going on in her life over the past few years. There was excitement in her voice and more energy than I remembered from earlier visits. After years of being a part-time student, the efforts finally paid off. Terri had completed her academic program and the college degree enabled her to get a good job. She felt more in control of her life than she had in years.

We did all the usual things. But there was something absent from our togetherness. Obviously missing was any reference to Robert. At most, his name came up in a few side comments. "Robert's okay." "Robert's working a lot of hours." "Robert's traveling a lot." There was nothing significant mentioned—nothing emotional. There were no statements about how *they* were doing or how she was feeling about their relationship. Discussing this area of her life was carefully avoided.

I wanted Terri to have the opportunity to talk about her marriage, but not as a result of pressure from me. So before we went to church, I mentioned the call from Robert and my interest in their well-being. I explained that if she wanted to talk, we could ride home in her car leaving the children to ride with Jan. She could think about it during the services. With the reluctance in Terri's eyes, I was a little surprised when she took me up on my offer.

The conversation that followed lasted well past the drive home. Terri confirmed Robert's fear. She was ready to leave the marriage. She had not as yet taken any legal steps, but she had sought the advice of an attorney.

Robert and I don't speak. It's not that he doesn't want to. I just refuse to talk to him. Our different work schedules have helped some. But there are still times when we're home together. I usually go to my room and avoid him completely.

I could probably stay in the marriage until the girls are older if he'd leave me alone. But that's not Robert's way. He wants it to be different. But it just can't. I don't want to talk to him or to even be around him. And I definitely don't want him touching me. I've had enough. It's over.

Terri seemed very resolute about her position. This was far different from the indecisive woman who sought my advice several years earlier. What had gotten her to this point? Had it been Robert's affair? I had seen many marriages survive the trauma created by extramarital involvement. So if it was the affair, it did not have to end this relationship. But was the affair really the problem?

Robert thinks I'm mad about the affair he had. He even had our pastor come by the house and talk with me about forgiveness and how it was my responsibility to take him back.

I admit that the affair hurt me quite a bit. Robert denied it for months until it was so obvious that he couldn't lie about it anymore. But my knowing didn't stop him. That's when we separated.

Robert continued to see her. I begged him to stop, but he wouldn't. That's what hurt me the most—my begging and his rejecting. Finally, it ended and Robert moved back home. Things have continued to deteriorate ever since.

Robert likes to point to the affair—or should I say, he likes to point to "my failure" to forgive him for having the affair—as the reason why I want out. But I really think I'm past that. It's not the affair.

I believed her. Though the affair was painful and damaging, I did not think it was causing the current crisis in their relationship. But if the affair and the hurt which it prompted were not the problem, then what was?

> The affair was only one part of our marriage. One part of a long history of events. I have finally realized that my real problem is with Robert. With who he is. With what he can and can't be in our marriage.
>
> Robert's not going to change. No matter what he says, and no matter what I do, our marriage will never be any different. Even now, he's saying some of the right things. He's admitting to some wrongdoing, but deep down he really doesn't see where any of this is his fault. It's still me—even with the affair. Robert doesn't think the real problem is with *his* having the affair. It's with *my* supposed unwillingness to forgive him. I can't win. I'm still the person *really* at fault. And that's the way he is.
>
> My marriage will always be the way it has been. Robert will always be controlling. He will always be demanding. He will always be selfish. I will always be the one in the wrong. And I will never feel safe, secure, or truly loved.
>
> When I finally came to that realization—that things would never be any different—I knew what I had to do. My choices became clear. I had to get out. I couldn't stay in it any longer.

There was a weariness in Terri's voice as we talked about her marriage. A definite change in her countenance compared to earlier in the weekend. Gone was the energy. Terri spoke in a monotone voice and her face was nearly expressionless. This subject was obviously draining. She seemed tired and worn-out.

Terri, there's something different about you. I've been
trying to figure out the difference as you've talked about your
marriage. It's occurred to me that your countenance is totally
different from what it's been over the past few days. You
seem to be dull . . . emotionally flat.

You've lost hope, haven't you? You've lost hope that your
marriage will ever be any different. That it will ever be stable;
that it will ever be caring; that it will ever be safe. You just
don't see any future in it—any hope for change.

There was a long pause in our conversation. Terri sat motionless
in the silence. She did not appear shocked or upset by what I had
said, only contemplative. She was thinking about my words in the
same manner that we sometimes take a breath, slowly, evaluating
each word, wanting to detect everything that was there. Then she
began to speak.

Yes. I believe you're right. "Hope" is the correct word
. . . for both what I think and how I feel. I have lost hope
. . . and I feel hopeless. My hope is totally gone.

Hope

"Hope" is not an unfamiliar term to most Christians. Usually, it is
thought of within a spiritual context. Hope is that part of our Christian
experience that *anticipates*. It looks forward (Titus 2:13). We have a
hope of a life to come (Titus 1:1-2). This hope is based on Jesus Christ,
the living God and Savior (1 Timothy 4:10) and our relationship
with Him (Colossians 1:27). Therefore, our hope is legitimate, not
illegitimate. It is true, not false. And it is certain, not uncertain.

Although hope is not of the present, but in anticipation of the future, it is always based on something. It is more than a mere whimsical notion. Our spiritual hope is based on the person Jesus Christ. It exudes from our relationship with Him—from the way we have learned to trust Him—from the loving ways He has intervened in our lives, either through changed circumstances or, when situations remained painfully unaltered, through His presence—and from how He has proven Himself faithful.

No mate can be as reliable as Jesus Christ. To think otherwise builds false security. In the best of situations, there would still be the hint of risk. But even though our surety in a mate cannot be as certain as our confidence in our Savior, a strong marital hope is both appropriate and essential.

Whether in our spiritual life or our marriage, however, hope springs from tangibles. It is always based on something. There is always a basis for our hope. And generally, this basis is experiential. It depends on what we have experienced, what we have found to be true.

Terri had lost hope. The words that she shared with me only confirmed what was visible in her eyes and evident in her voice. She was defeated. Dashed were her dreams, as if they had been pounded by the sea. Gone was any anticipation of a future marked with safety and caring. Instead, she only saw more of what had been already painfully experienced: insensitivity, selfishness, and forceful control. There was nothing that maintained a hope. So she finally gave it up.

Robert was correct in feeling desperate. He was in a desperate situation. Without hope, a marriage fails. And Terri had lost hers. Slowly, but effectively, it had been taken from her. There seemed to be little remaining to be done other than offering the official pronouncement for the cause of death: *Death by reason of lost hope.*

Theirs was a marriage in crisis. As such, it faced the very real possibility of ending. My friends' relationship could become another statistic. But as desperate as things appeared, their marriage was not yet beyond the realm of restoration. It could still be saved.

With the loss of hope, their relationship entered a crisis. With hope's return would come *opportunity*. There would be opportunity for *reconciliation* (forgiveness and healing). There would also be opportunity for *restoration* (building back and building up). But the occurrence of either of these would only be possible with the return of hope.

Hope can return to Robert and Terri's marriage. And with it will come the opportunity for reconciliation and restoration. But true hope has a basis. There must be something tangible. Hope will only return for their relationship if Robert can give Terri a legitimate reason to believe that things can be different. He will have to give her a reason for hope. And for Robert, this will undoubtedly require a genuine *change of heart*.

What was getting Robert in trouble was his behavior. He was abusive and controlling. But behavior is strongly connected to attitude. Robert had a need to exert control over Terri and saw nothing wrong with treating her in any manner deemed necessary to achieve this goal. For Robert, there would have to be a change of heart before there would be any true and lasting change in his behavior.

Probably no one recognized the connection between a change of heart and a change in behavior more clearly than the apostle Paul. Think of the impact that a heart changed on the road to Damascus has had on Christendom today. Paul wrote to Timothy about the need for a change of heart in some of the brethren in his time. He was not referring to husbands and wives. Still, he was clearly addressing the needs of those whose behavior was in need of correction. Regarding these needy brethren, Paul shared with Timothy his concern that:

> The Lord may grant them *a change of heart* and show them the truth, and thus they may come to their senses and escape the devil's snare . . .
>
> 2 Timothy 2:25(b)-26(a)

Paul was suggesting that a *behavior problem* is frequently a *heart problem*. Change the heart and the behavior will adapt. That's not bad psychology. Change Robert's heart, and his behavior will change. Change Robert's heart, and hope may return for Terri. Change Robert's heart, and possibly their marriage will be saved.

Terri had experienced a great deal of emotional pain. Being married to Robert had taken its toll in many ways, not the least of which was an assault on her own self-esteem. But there was nothing that a genuinely changed heart and truly changed behavior could not potentially restore.

I believe that God always has a future for His people—regardless of the situation or circumstances. Robert may not have a change of heart. Hope may not necessarily return to the marriage. Reconciliation and restoration may not occur. But even in these circumstances, for the Christian, there is always hope. We may lose our hope for the marriage. But there is always hope in the Lord and in His power to bring sufficiency to our lives. Whether doing all that we know to do results in moving "in" to the marriage or "on" with life, God always has a future for His people.

Whether we are dealing with Terri and Robert's marriage, or any other marriage where the healthy anticipation of the future is waning, there is a way hope can be restored. But it will require effort. Far too often, we want circumstances to be changed without our having to personally deal with them. We expect a quick fix. We want a miraculous intervention from the Lord to heal or rectify our situation. This desire to be relieved of any responsibility is understandable. But it is not realistic. Nor is it the Lord's design.

There is a biblical plan for dealing with marriages that have lost hope. Seemingly hopeless relationships can be saved. But the Lord will not do for us what we can do for ourselves. Change will not come without effort. Hope can be restored but it will require our taking responsibility for our situation. With the restoration of legitimate hope will come the opportunity for a truly reconciled relationship. **When mates have a change of heart, God's power for restoration and healing is revealed.**

2

Not All the Same Story

The difference between lost and losing is a matter of degrees. Whereas Terri had lost hope in the future of her marriage, Judy was losing hers. She was still in the process.

It had been several months since the last time I had seen Judy and John. I can't say that I knew them well. We had only met together for a few sessions. John had been reluctant for him and Judy to come for counseling at all and was totally disapproving of Judy's seeking help on her own. So, they dropped out. But now we were six months further into the marriage and Judy was again in my office. This time without John.

> I knew John wouldn't come back when we were sitting here in your office last time. I could tell by the expression on his face. He didn't like what he was hearing, from either you or me.

John was a good man, and Judy was the first to acknowledge that. In fact, some of her guilt for being dissatisfied with the marriage revolved around this very issue of John's goodness. He was stable and dependable, a good provider, and a godly man. But he didn't understand Judy and he had difficulties with her needs. I remember John's initial assessment of his marriage.

> We are truly blessed. We have everything we need and most of what we want. I am happy with myself, with Judy, with my son, and with my job. What more could I ask?
>
> I feel Judy, though, is unhappy. She gets aggravated at herself and takes it out on me.

John was a genuinely nice guy. That wasn't hard to see. But the more I talked with him, the more apparent it became that he might not be the easiest man to live with. He was nice. But he was also very traditional. I found him frequently referring to Judy's role and of her "call."

> The Lord has called Judy to a Christian mother's role which requires self-discipline. He has also called her to be the best wife she can be. I think she feels inadequate in these roles.
>
> We've been working on these since we got married. Judy's made a lot of improvement, but she continues to have a problem with independence. It goes back to her family life. Judy was raised in a family where she had to assume a lot of responsibility. Her father wasn't very dependable and her mother was weak. Judy had to be pretty independent just to survive. Now, it's hard for her to let go of that independent attitude and be dependent upon a man, even if it's her husband.

Judy's supposed independent attitude was displayed by the fact that she had interests beyond those of domestic activities. She liked being a homemaker and loved the dimension of life that having a son brought to her. But Judy also had other interests. Judy had pursued a career before marriage. Though she had no desire to reenter the job market on a full-time basis, she needed more diversity in her life than was offered by staying at home. This desire for diversity, and her failure to be totally content with domestic responsibilities, is what John viewed as strong independence.

> It's important to me to have a comfortable, non-chaotic home. I believe it's what the Lord wants. I need Judy's support in this. She is responsible for the home. It is her job to see that our son is cared for, the clothes are done, the meals prepared, and the house kept clean. That's what the Lord has called her to do. All that the Lord expects of Judy is for her to be a good Christian wife and mother. And that's all I expect, too—nothing more and nothing less.
>
> Judy's doing a better job. She just needs a little more organization. She says she wants to be organized, but she doesn't seem to have pride in her work.

There is nothing wrong with traditional thinking. But it can be pushed to an extreme. One way of pushing it to an extreme edge is by rigidly defining traditional roles as either the only "correct" roles or the only "godly" roles. That's what was happening here. For John, roles for husbands and wives were clearly defined. And there was no room for deviation. To be different was to be deviant. Therefore, to be different was not acceptable. The problem was not with John's traditionalism. It was with his unwillingness to allow any other position.

It was not difficult determining how John developed his perspective on family life. He was raised in a very traditional home where "responsible" was the operative word. A household that was calm, routine, and orderly was the expectation. John's father successfully operated the family business. But like many other success stories, it was very timeconsuming. There was little opportunity for him and John to be together. "He loved me, but he had no time for me. Dad really wasn't an emotional kind of guy."

John's mother was a more constant figure during the years of his growing up. She was a very giving person when it came to tangibly helping friends and neighbors, and she also did a better job of showing John love than his father did. However, she was also very busy and could not be accurately described as a nurturer. "Mom was more concerned with the house being clean than spending time with us (the children)."

As John talked, it became clear that he came by his perspectives of family life honestly. He liked the roles he had learned at home. Not only in the behavioral expectations of husband and wife or father and mother, but also in the manner in which people relate emotionally. John, much like both of his parents, described himself as a "private person." Keeping his feelings to himself, he was not inclined to share them. And what's more, he didn't really understand the needs of others in this area. Responsible, perfunctory, "just the facts ma'am" . . . that's the way John liked it. That's what made him comfortable. And that's the way it was *supposed* to be.

When Judy first came for counseling, it was with the goal of trying to further change herself. Being told that she had a problem with rebellion gradually made her a believer. If only she could give up her need for independence and her expectation for a marriage with more than sterile relationships, things would be fine. I got into trouble with John when I began to move the focus of the problem away from Judy and a spiritual nature to their relationship and the adjustments it needed. To John, this was not very good Christian counsel. It was this redefinition of the problem that prompted the premature end to our meeting some six months earlier.

But here we were, a half a year further into the marital journey, with Judy alone in my office. What had changed? Were things better? Were they worse? And why was Judy in my office at this particular time instead of a month earlier or a month later? What precipitated her return to counseling?

> I can't tell you the sense of relief that came over me when you told us our problem wasn't a spiritual problem. It was as if a tremendous burden had been lifted off of me. I could breathe again. It made so much sense.
>
> After five years of "working on Judy"—trying to deal with my apparent lack of submission to both God's role design and John's role expectations—I suddenly realized that my preferences were not the problem. There was nothing wrong with what I wanted for myself or my marriage.
>
> I'm sorry to say that John still refuses to see it that way. He persists in viewing *the* problem as *my* problem. For John, the problem continues to be my unwillingness to yield to God's design.

What prompted Judy's return was an incident with her son. Judy was aware that her unhappiness with John's rigidity and nonacceptance had been increasing. But she had resigned herself to the situation. She had the hope that if she could only give enough, and be nice enough, and hold on long enough, things might change. Judy had no idea that anyone else was being affected. Then her son started behaving differently. A trip to their pediatrician brought the following analysis. "There's stress in his life. I don't know what it is, but you'd better deal with it."

That was enough for Judy to break out of her equilibrium. She decided to visit her parents for a week just to see what changes it brought. Judy found that while she was away from home, her mood improved. There was no sense of pressure—no cleaning schedules to meet in order to keep John content—no meals that had to be served at a specific time. Things were more relaxed. And her son's behavior responded accordingly. He was his old self. It seemed that Judy's context had been more stressful than even she had realized. Judy then returned home and began making some changes in her lifestyle. One of the changes was to return to counseling.

> I'm afraid things are deteriorating for John and me. But he refuses to understand why. I love him—and I desperately want our marriage—but I fear for its future.

The following statements were sprinkled throughout our conversation.

- I can't meet John's expectations. No matter how hard I try, I can't measure up.

- Emotionally, I'm dying on the vine. He's totally oblivious to my emotional needs. The only kind of closeness which John wants is sexual.

- John refuses to accept me for who I am. As long as I do what he wants, he is perfectly happy with the marriage. But the minute I disagree or talk about a different way of looking at something, he says I'm resisting God's design for my life.

- I entered the marriage with a pretty good self-esteem. Now, it's worse. That's a terrible thing to say about marriage. It's not supposed to be that way.

Judy was a young wife and mother with legitimate needs and expectations. She loved her husband and wanted her marriage to last. John was a good man who loved his wife. He too wanted his marriage to last. But they differed on what this marriage was to look like. We're not talking about deviancy. We're merely talking about differences. But, whereas Judy was willing to talk about their differences and work on adjustments, John was not. It had to be his way . . . the only "correct and godly" way.

As I sat and listened to Judy, I was struck by the extent to which people subject themselves to unnecessary pain. There are many things that confront us over which we have no control. I have no influence over death and taxes. I can't determine the economic future of the country, whether there will be a recession or whether industry will prosper. Much of my life is taken one day at a time. Just like you, I deal with what comes my way. But one area of my life where I do have some influence is my marriage. Obviously, I can't totally control a relationship. Nor would I want to. But I can be responsible for my part. And that has quite an influence on my marriage as a whole. By taking responsibility for my part, and Jan doing likewise for hers, we avoid a great deal of unnecessary pain.

Much of the pain that Judy and John were experiencing was absolutely unnecessary. Their struggle didn't have to be happening. True, their marriage was not close to ending. And even if there was no change in its present course, it would be some time before Judy would totally lose hope. She would have to experience more insensitivity, more misunderstanding, more rejection, more encounters with John's tendency to be emotionally closed, and more pressure to fit into a particular mold. But eventually, unless something changed for her and John, Judy would likely reach a point where hope would be gone. She would give up on the future being any different. John would have sucked her dry. Then, having lost hope, their marriage would enter a crisis. And it all would be unnecessary.

Marital Extremes

I work with marital extremes. If you were to look at a continuum with healthy, growing, stable, and vibrant marriages on one end and relationships in crisis on the other, it is the marriages in crisis which I most frequently see. These are the relationships which generally come to counseling. From this vantage point, the marriage of Terri and Robert definitely qualified as one that was in trouble. Terri had lost hope. Their relationship was in crisis. It could be listed among the extremes. But in my years as a marital therapist, I have learned that *extremes are merely situations which have reached the end of a journey*.

Terri and Robert did not start out on their marital journey as an extreme. Their marriage did not begin in crisis. They entered marriage much like the rest of us, with enthusiasm and optimism for the future. But things began to change. Event by event, their relationship traveled in a hazardous direction. Finally, Terri lost hope.

Terri and Robert's marriage had actually been failing for quite some time. But it was not until Terri *lost hope* that their relationship entered a crisis. Then they became an extreme.

There are many couples who do not see themselves categorized with Terri and Robert. They do not see themselves as having lost hope. Like Judy and John, they are not yet numbered among the extremes. But, they are en route. Hope is not lost, but it is being lost. For these couples, the journey is not yet complete. There are more roads to be taken—more hazards to be encountered—more pain—more disappointments—more disillusionment. But unless the direction is changed, they too will succumb to the same fate. Hope will ultimately be lost. And they too will be counted among the extremes.

Variations

Marriages in the process of losing hope do not all have the same appearance. There are variations in how hope is lost. At least, there are variations in the more cosmetic features.

Two common conceptions about lost-hope marriages are: 1) they are extremely pathological, and 2) they are very noticeable. Though these two perceptions are accurate for many of the relationships where hope is lost, they are not true for all. While some relationships are marked with severe behavioral excesses or deficits, others are fairly normal. And while in some relationships the failing condition is very noticeable, others proceed with little or no fanfare. There are differences in how we fail.

Sometimes, there is abnormality. In one form or another, these relationships are marred by deviant behavior—behavior that is unacceptable regardless of the context. An example of this would be the physical abuse of a mate. This is inappropriate behavior regardless of the motivation or perceived justification. There is no right reason for doing the wrong thing. And that is no truer than in the area of spouse physical abuse.

Spouse abuse is not limited to a physical nature. A mate can be abusive and never lift a hand. I have seen many self esteems bludgeoned beyond recognition by mere words. Did I say "mere" words? Words are powerful. And used in a demeaning and harassing manner, their potency can create emotional scars that last as long as any wounds inflicted on the body.

This type of abnormality speaks to the issue of *safety*. It is hard to feel safe in an abusive environment—a home where fear of threat to self or others is constant. Another type of abnormality speaks to the issue of *security*. This is generally demonstrated through various forms of irresponsibility. Sometimes this irresponsibility takes the form of an addiction. Whether the particular substance of choice be something as tangible as alcohol, drugs, and food, or as intangible as gambling and sex, the consequence for the marriage is the same. The unabated pursuit of an external commodity, solely for building a false sense of self-satisfaction, does nothing but wreak havoc on a household. Gone is order. Gone is predictability. Gone is accountability. And gone is security.

Irresponsibility can extend beyond obvious obsessions. Sometimes it's not what you do, but what you don't do that creates the loss of hope. One of the more frustrated wives that I have ever met had little complaint about what her husband did. He was neither abusive toward her nor addicted to any substance. Rather, he simply would not work. Any job that he began he promptly quit. If he did not actually walk off on his own, his performance would be so poor and inconsistent that a frustrated employer would finally have to dismiss him. This husband was content to sit at home and allow his wife to support the family, whether through her own employment or assistance she obtained through social service programs. He aptly demonstrated that non-behavior can be as irresponsible as misbehavior.

Obsessions do not always have a pathological look. We have mentioned the obvious addictions. What about those of a more subtle nature—those with an appearance of legitimacy? One case that immediately comes to mind is the workaholic. This is a person, man or woman, who is obsessed with his job. Work is his passion. This is where his energy is spent, both physical and emotional. These marriages are not marred by insecurity as much as they are by neglect. Amidst what may be an external appearance of stability, the internal structure of the relationship crumbles. There is no emotional investment so the marriage fails to thrive. It literally dries up. That is a high price to pay for career success.

We have been discussing some extreme situations. Anytime you are dealing with abusive, addictive, or obsessive behavior, you are dealing with extremes. This was Terri's situation. Robert was verbally abusive. He was also very controlling. But make no mistake: not every situation will be glaring and pathological. It will not necessarily be for lack of either safety or security that all marriages lose hope. Some will lose hope for saner reasons and with saner, more ordinary mates. Such was the case with Judy.

John had his own set of quirks and idiosyncrasies. Like most of us, there were chinks in his armor. There were areas in his personality that merited improvement. John could have been more flexible. He could have been more concerned about Judy's needs instead of rigidly holding to his own. And he could have been more open emotionally. Instead of being a private person and keeping his feelings to himself, he could have been expressive and sharing. But be this as it may, he was not pathological. For the most part, John would fall into the same category as you and I. He would fit that grouping of people referred to as "ordinary." But even though ordinary, he was still in a marriage that was losing hope.

Ordinary people in ordinary relationships can lose hope, too. Usually this occurs when legitimate expectations for marital health are not met. It is legitimate to expect the investment of time and energy to take place. It is legitimate to expect mates to share who they are with one another—to talk about how they feel and what they think—to be self-disclosing. It is legitimate to expect bonding in a marriage—to grow together. When marital health is the expectation and, whether through insensitivity or avoidance or neglect, it fails to happen, even ordinary people begin to lose hope. And when ordinary people in ordinary marriages lose hope, their relationships will also enter crisis.

3

A Progressive Problem

One reason for looking at a marriage like Judy and John's is to eliminate any preconceived notions regarding the kind of relationships which lose hope. Sometimes we think that only those of extreme conditions are destined to deteriorate in this manner. We assume that only the truly disturbed have problems. While deviant and pathological behavior can rob a marriage of safety and security, and ultimately of hope itself, this can also be the destination of ordinary relationships, inhabited by ordinary people. It is a possibility which you and I must also guard against.

There are differences in relationships. Marriages do not all have the same look. But as important as these differences may be, there is a real sense that these variations are only cosmetic in nature. Amidst the idiosyncratic differences, there is always a commonality in the manner in which hope is lost. Pervasive and consistent similarities run through these marriages. Regardless of the unique characteristics which serve to distinguish these relationships from one another, the *cycle* of deterioration is the same for all.

The Cycle of Losing Hope

In some respects, referring to the loss of hope as a cycle is probably not the most accurate description. We usually save this term for sequences like the seasons. Autumn, winter, spring, and summer are always present during a year. They are predictable and they are always in the same order. The presence of specified elements, and a preestablished sequence or order, are two characteristics which are consistent with most definitions of a cycle. A final characteristic, however, is the tendency for repetitive action. The cycle of the seasons will not only occur once, but will recur time and time again. The repetitive nature of the entire sequence is predictable.

The characteristics which lead to the loss of hope are as predictable as the seasons. They are clearly identifiable and routinely follow one another in a prescribed sequence. However, this is not a sequence that is likely to repeat itself, time after time, in the same relationship. Thus, this is the deviation from a true cycle. In a marriage, you may only get one chance.

There is unacceptable behavior

The first element in the cycle of lost hope is the presence of unacceptable behavior. In some instances, this behavior will be clearly inappropriate. This is the case with extremely deviant behaviors such as abuse and addiction. But unacceptable behavior is not limited to the extremes of deviancy. The continuum covers less malignant, yet still undesirable, actions. Such was the case with David and Donna.

At our first session, David and Donna represented a contrast in countenance. David sat very erect in his chair. He was tense and anxious. Donna, on the other hand, slouched in hers. Actually, she was nearly reclining. Leaning to one side, the chair was barely able to contain her posture. It was not that she was relaxed as in cool, calm, and collected. Rather, it was more the posture of a person who was totally worn-out. She looked tired. As we worked through the session, it became apparent just how tired she was.

> I don't know what I'm willing to do. I've been giving and giving for fifteen years. For the past two years I've tried to get David to come to counseling. Now it may be too late. I just don't know if I've got anything left to give. And even if I did, I certainly don't know what good it would do.

Donna looked drained. There didn't seem to be an ounce of energy left in her. And what was the behavior that prompted her response? What was David's errancy? Was it abusive behavior? Was it a personal addiction? No. In fact, it was nothing even close to being that drastic. The problem was David's tendency to avoid conflict. He simply would not deal with any dissatisfactions which arose in the marriage. Though far less malignant in appearance, however, it was still unacceptable behavior for Donna.

> David won't deal with me. If there's something that he's unhappy about, he just stuffs it. If there's something that I'm dissatisfied with, any attempt that I make to talk to him about it is totally avoided. He simply will not deal with me about anything that has the potential for conflict. Consequently, nothing gets resolved. I find that so frustrating.
>
> It's broader than just me. He avoids other stressful situations also. I've been watching over his shoulder for the entire fifteen years of our marriage—making sure he deals with taxes—making sure he deals with creditors when money is tight. It is David's history. He really does not like dealing with anything that's stressful.

> I understand the discomfort that comes from having to
> deal with threatening situations. But avoidance is no solution.
> I'm tired of living this way. I can't live this way. I won't live
> this way. I'm through.

These were strong words. But Donna probably had even stronger feelings. Both the words and the feelings were prompted by unacceptable behavior. This behavior was not deviant, but it was unacceptable nonetheless.

There is a continuum for behavior—a continuum with deviancy on one end and non-deviancy on the other. A key issue which transcends this continuum is *legitimacy*. Determining what is a legitimate expectation helps to make sense out of our confusion. How can a behavior be non-deviant and still be considered unacceptable? Simple. At least, it's simple when you realize that just because a behavior misses the realm of pathology and instead, falls somewhere in the range of normality, does not necessarily make it beneficial and constructive to a relationship. This seems to be the pivotal distinction. Is the behavior beneficial and constructive? If it is, then good. If it is not, however, then not so good. It is legitimate to expect healthy behavior from a mate. But it is equally legitimate to be non-accepting of unhealthy behavior. Whether the behavior be glaringly deviant as in the case of addiction, or less malignant as in the case of avoidance, neither one is acceptable because neither one is constructive.

It is legitimate to expect health in a relationship. It is legitimate to expect safety. It is legitimate to expect security. It is legitimate to expect a mate to be responsible and accountable. It is legitimate to expect shared responsibility in the home. It is legitimate to expect the investment of time into the relationship. It is legitimate to expect emotional honesty. It is legitimate to expect that a mate deal directly with conflict—to not be avoidant. And it is legitimate to expect self-disclosure—for a mate to talk about how he feels and what he thinks. All of this is healthy. All of this is constructive. All of this is legitimate. And it is behavior that is also legitimate to expect.

For the purpose of this book, I want to define two labels. With this cycle of losing hope, there is always unacceptable behavior. One mate acts as the offender and the other is the offended. For simplicity's sake, the mate who is behaving unacceptably will be referred to as the *offender* and the marital partner who is the recipient of this behavior will be referred to as the *spouse*. This labeling will help reduce confusion about who is doing what.

Within a marriage that is losing hope, the message that is given off by the offender's unacceptable behavior is, "You don't count." John's behavior was different from that of Robert's. One bordered on being abnormal whereas, the other did not. But the message transmitted was the same for both. And whether behavior is selfish, self-serving, self-protective, totally deviant, or within the bounds of normality, the message ultimately becomes a greater problem than the action itself.

Nothing strikes at the heart of a relationship more significantly than insensitivity to need. It erodes the very foundation of a marriage. And this is regardless of intent. Sometimes inappropriate behavior is not intentionally meant to be insensitive. It is much easier to identify behavior than it is to determine motivation. Calculating the "whats" is easier than the "whys." But frequently, this makes little difference. A behavior is seen and then it is given meaning. This meaning then becomes our reality. And when behavior transmits a statement of "I don't care about what you want or need," even if this perceived message is not totally accurate, the marriage begins to fail.

The first characteristic of the cycle of lost hope is unacceptable behavior. Whether clearly deviant or only mildly undesirable, the bounds of legitimacy will be crossed. And with the crossing of this boundary, we are ready for the next step of our journey.

There is a pattern

The second characteristic of the cycle of losing hope is the existence of a pattern. By pattern I mean there is repetition. **Hope does not leave a marriage because of a lone incident or event.** It takes more than that. Hope is far too resilient. Though the action itself may be bad enough, it is really the repetitive nature of the unacceptable behavior that causes the damage.

The term used by Donna to articulate this in her marriage was "history." She kept referring to David's history of avoidance. That was a very apt description. David did not avoid Donna on only one occasion. Nor was it merely two or three incidences. She said he "totally" avoided her. For David, avoidance had a repetitive aspect. It was a pattern. The unacceptable behavior in a marriage that loses hope always has a historical nature. It has a past tense. It has a present tense. And unfortunately for the relationship, the spouse believes that it also has a future tense.

There are terms that are used to help describe differences in patterns. For instance, sometimes a behavior is reported as constant. Another behavior may be episodic. Usually these terms are purposed at describing how frequently a particular behavior may be occurring. In reality, the only difference between these descriptions is the length of time between incidences. The history and the repetitive nature are still there. And it is the pattern, not necessarily the frequency, that is the problem. With each execution, a little more hope is siphoned off from what remains.

Think back to the previous illustrations. In all of them there has been unacceptable behavior. Sometimes this behavior had a more malignant nature. That was the case with Terri and Robert. Theirs was a marriage characterized by coercion, control, and abuse. Sometimes this behavior was less extreme. We witnessed that with Judy and John where John's rigid non-acceptance of Judy's needs proved to be problematic. But in each case, the behavior was repetitive. The offender did not act once, but again and again. In marriages that lose hope, this is the norm. A repetitive pattern of offending behavior is always present.

There is a progressive deterioration

The final element in the cycle of losing hope is the progressive deterioration of the relationship. Actually, deterioration isn't really a step that follows after the other two as much as it is a companion that goes along for the ride. The further the trip, however, the more dominant a companion deterioration becomes.

Deterioration is progressive. The foothold is established with the first appearance of the unacceptable behavior. There is a first time for abuse. There is a first time for forceful control. There is a first time for non-acceptance. And there is a first time for avoidance. Then, with each subsequent execution of the characteristic behavior, the pattern unfolds and the problem grows larger. Progressively, deterioration looms over the marriage.

We can see this more clearly with Terri and Robert. Their relationship has been chronicled from start to finish. With the passage of time, Terri progressively got to the place where her statement was: "I've had enough. It's over." Though Donna and David reported a far less malignant history, this was also the place where Donna arrived: "I'm tired of living this way. I can't live this way. I won't live this way. I'm through." Both of these relationships reflect ordinary beginnings and extraordinary endings. What began with legitimate hopes and expectations gradually and progressively arrived at a point of crisis. Someone finally said; "Enough is enough. I'm tired of what's going on."

Judy and John illustrate what it is like to be *in* the cycle but not yet *through* the cycle. Do you remember Judy's statement?

> I'm afraid things are deteriorating for John and me. But he refuses to understand why. I love him—and I desperately want our marriage—but I fear for its future.

Judy and John have not progressed as far as the other two couples. Their marriage will require a little more time. Given enough time, and with no change in the current pattern, the progressive nature of the cycle for losing hope in a marriage will likely claim another victim.

The progressive nature of deterioration is summarized by the subtle change in a statement. At the beginning, the statement made by unacceptable behavior is "You don't count." One incident alone is damaging enough to a relationship. The pattern characteristic of this cycle only serves to worsen the situation by repetitively counter-sinking this message deep into the psyche of the spouse. Ultimately, the message begins to change. What started as "You don't count" expands to include the additional closing comment, "and you won't ever count." It is when the message reaches this final transformation, which is a progressive change, that hope departs. Progressively, the marriage reaches a point of crisis.

Losing hope is progressive. It doesn't happen because of an incident. It requires a pattern. The repetitive execution of unacceptable behavior gradually takes its toll. And as we will now see, the consequence of this deterioration is significant.

4

Giving Up

When hope departs from a marriage, there is not much that remains. Far too clearly, the illustrations which we have already witnessed have borne the truth of this statement. The structure of the marriage may be there—the shell—the institution. But the relationship itself—the emotional aspect—has dissipated.

When hope is gone, all that seems to be left is *resignation*. At long last, after years of progressive and methodical movement through the degenerating cycle, the spouse finally resigns himself or herself to the conclusion that the marriage will get no better. Please note that I did not say the spouse resigns himself or herself to the "fact" that the marriage will get no better. The thought that the marriage will get no better may not necessarily be fact. Nevertheless, this is the conclusion that is believed. And armed with this belief, a resigned spouse from a multiple-year marriage finally gives up.

When a spouse gives up on a marriage, he stops working at it. This was demonstrated in Terri's marriage by her refusal to even talk to her husband. Terri wanted to have nothing to do with Robert. She was through. She wanted to make no further efforts toward reconciliation or restoration. All that Terri did want was for Robert to leave her alone. "I don't want to talk to him or to even be around him. And I definitely don't want him touching me. I've had enough. It's over."

Donna expressed a similar sentiment regarding her situation with David. "I don't know what I'm willing to do. . . . Now it may be too late. I just don't know if I've got anything left to give. And even if I did, I certainly don't know what good it would do." Donna, like Terri, had given up. She had quit. The willingness to make concessions was gone. The desire to do something constructive was no longer there. One thing that Terri and Donna shared in common was a vocabulary—a vocabulary that omitted words like "continue" and "effort." Their real desire was no longer to continue in well-doing or to make valiant efforts—it was to do nothing.

This tendency to quit is precisely the reason why hope is so essential to a relationship. Hope gives us energy. It gives us power. Hope drives us. It is the force which makes possible the opportunity for creative adaptation. Note that I said it gives us the "opportunity" for creative adaptation. Not all of us will take advantage of this opportunity. Sometimes, hope only gives us the power to passively "hang-on." Nevertheless, without it, a relationship becomes lifeless—the "want to" departs. And with the departure of this power source goes the opportunity for change. Thus, the sentiments expressed by Terri and Donna, "I'm through . . . I have nothing left to give," take on understanding. These spouses quit because they had no more energy. And they had no more energy because they had no more hope.

When spouses finally give up—when they finally lose hope—

when their energy is finally depleted—and when they finally quit trying—they find themselves at one of four destinations. I refer to these destinations as *stations*. As we will soon discover, even in giving up, there are differences.

The Four Stations of Lost Hope

Stations are not to be confused with stages. When referring to stages, we are describing growth plateaus which are developmental and sequential. For example, children will naturally move from one predictable stage to another until they finally reach adulthood. We call this maturation. It is important that each stage be visited. At each stage, there are tasks to be accomplished and skills to be learned. This preparation is needed so that a child is ready to then move on. One stage always precedes, thus leading the way to, the next.

Moving from one plateau to the next is not the case with stations. Like stages, each station has its own uniqueness. There are characteristics which distinguish one station from the others. But there is no sequence involved. You do not start with one station and then predictably move to the next. There can be movement from station to station. But if this occurs, it is based solely on the uniqueness of the individual and his particular situation, and not on any grand developmental plan. An individual may move back and forth between two stations, repeating this movement for years, or make absolutely no movement at all. I have known some spouses to lose hope, settle into a particular station, and remain there for years throughout the duration of their marriage.

Stations are my way of differentiating hopelessness. Though those who lose hope hold in common the lack of anticipation for a better marital future, this hopelessness will be played out in different ways. Stations are the postures or stances which these spouses will assume. Each will have its own peculiarities—its own characteristics. Some will be better than others. But none will be good.

Despair

The characteristic which most distinguishes despair from the other stations is its emotional intensity. Spouses in despair are on the jagged edge. Their emotions are frayed. Though the particular distress can be varied, it will usually include at least one of the following symptoms: anxiety, depression, helplessness, a sense of entrapment, intense anger, frustration, or resentment. Frequently, the despair becomes so severe that the spouse is prompted to seek some kind of therapeutic help. It was just this kind of despair that brought Gwen to my office.

Gwen and Steven had been married for thirteen years. They entered marriage with an appropriate degree of optimism. But over the past five years, Gwen watched the early expectations and anticipations of what her life would be like slowly dwindle away. Finally, Gwen lost hope. She entered the station of despair when Steven was laid off from his job.

> This makes the fourth time in our marriage that Steven has been laid off. The last time it happened, he just sat around waiting to be called back. Steven didn't begin looking for something else until the unemployment money stopped coming in.
>
> I am so frustrated with my life. Here I am, thirty-five years old, and financially dependent upon my parents. I guess I should be thankful that they're able to help us. But it's so embarrassing. We have no house of our own and don't seem

to be making any headway toward one. Steven just sits around and says, "It'll all work out. Don't worry."

Well, I'm tired of sitting and waiting and doing nothing. I was all set to go back to school and at least do something with my life when Steven got laid off again. That was the last straw. I've gone back to work with a temporary service to help out with the finances. But Steven's still sitting and waiting.

Gwen was more than frustrated. She was intensely angry and depressed. She cried during most of the session. Trapped and overwhelmed, Gwen saw no way out of her situation. And she had totally lost confidence in Steven's ability to lead and care for the family.

I feel as though I've got three kids to raise instead of two. Steven doesn't follow through on anything. He'll start a project and then just stop. It won't be finished. But that doesn't seem to bother him. After stepping over and around things for a few weeks, I'll finally get mad enough to get upset at him. This usually gets him working on it again. But even then, there's no guarantee it will get done.

Steven was not an uncaring and insensitive ogre. To the contrary, he was actually quite nice and pleasant. But he was not what I would call impressive. Steven was used to being taken care of. That's what his mother and older sisters had done for most of his life. Why should marriage be any different? Insensitive and uncaring? No, these were not good descriptive terms for Steven. Far better words would be passive, avoidant, and inept. Be that as it may, these were characteristics which Gwen had long grown tired of.

Gwen wanted Steven to take more control of his life. She wanted him to demonstrate some initiative. His passivity frustrated her. She needed to sense more security in their situation. During a session when they were both meeting with me, I asked Steven to explain to Gwen his plan for dealing with their stressful situation. This seemed to make him nervous. He rambled for a few minutes but basically said nothing new. His plan was just to continue sitting and waiting. When Steven stopped talking, the room grew silent. Gwen just looked down at the floor. Finally, I asked Gwen what she was thinking and feeling. Slowly, she looked up and began to cry. After a few moments, Gwen began to respond to Steven's comments.

> I feel I am willing to do whatever it takes to deal with our situation. I've gone to work instead of staying home with the children. And if need be, I'd get a second job. But I don't feel you're willing to do the same. And that makes me furious.

Gwen was in the station of despair. She was angry, depressed, and she felt trapped. Part of this was due to her loss of hope; part was due to the stressful circumstances; and part was due to the individual uniqueness found in both hers and Steven's personalities. But regardless of the factors which contributed to her arrival at this particular posture, the distinguishing characteristic of emotional intensity was clearly present. Gwen was in distress.

Some of my colleagues have suggested that despair is a station which all of those who lose hope must pass through. They suggest despair is a hub. Passage through despair is required before admission to any of the other stations can be attained. I am not so sure. Many spouses do enter despair—but not all. And those who do find this station tend to not tarry there long. The pain is too great. A spouse in despair may move to another station. Or, out of desperation, he may move out of the marriage entirely. He may even be motivated to deal with the marriage in such a manner as to allow hope to return. But remaining in despair is not likely to be an option.

Defeat

If emotional intensity is the distinguishing characteristic for the station of despair, just the opposite is the hallmark for the station of defeat. A defeated spouse is emotionless. His countenance is dull, bland, and void of expression. He just exists, lethargic.

We have already witnessed two examples of defeated mates. The first was Terri. I described her as weary and tired—as appearing to be physically worn-out. Her expressions were lifeless. She spoke in a monotone voice as if she had been numbed by life. Donna was another example of defeat. She, too, appeared drained. "There didn't seem to be an ounce of energy left in her." Donna was emotionally flat and verbalized how she had nothing left to give.

This absence of emotion is the station of defeat. For Terri, it was a second stop. Earlier in her marriage, she had visited despair. But self-preservation began to set in. Gradually, the emotional intensity departed and she became numb. The station of defeat was not a good position, but it was preferable to that of despair. With it came relief from being constantly overwhelmed by emotions. There is something to be said for any shelter in the midst of an emotional storm.

Though this was a progressive move for Terri, it was a port of entry for Donna. She had found David's avoidant behavior to be frustrating, but not to the point of despair. And though his behavior still served to cause some frustration, her basic emotional tone was flat. Donna, like Terri, serves to illustrate the station of defeat.

Disregard

The stations of despair and defeat were easily and succinctly described. The primary theme for both centers around a single element. For despair, the focus is on the intensity of emotion; for defeat it is the lack of emotion. Compared to these two previous stations, disregard is far more complex. There are many facets to what has proven to be the most enduring of the stations.

One of the distinguishing characteristics of this station is the willingness to bargain. The spouse loses hope in the future of the marriage. The conclusion that things will be no different is reached and realized. But with the realization is an acceptance. The marital disappointment which comes from frustrated expectations can be accepted as long as there is some significant payoff. "As long as I benefit, things will be okay." Usually, this personal gain is tangible and centers around themes like comfort, security, stability, and status. A lesser life is "settled for," but it is a lesser life with means.

A disregarding spouse establishes a separate life. The marriage seems to function well enough. The mates are typically civil to one another and the perfunctory tasks of running a home are handled. There is even the external appearance of marital stability. But there is little internal bonding or connectedness. Each mate does as he pleases with little thought or consideration for the needs and desires of the other. A common attitude of discounting is present: "I'll do what I want in spite of your wishes. Regardless of your needs, I will do as I please."

What naturally accompanies the establishment of separate lives is a list of personal priorities—areas of investment which serve as replacements for the marriage. These usually include legitimate activities such as career, children, recreational interests, and even the church. It is not unusual for a disregarding spouse's investment in one of these areas to be excessive. Remember, this was not the first choice. It is a substitute. And for the substitute to keep on doing its job as a void-filler, an over-involvement is almost always required.

This concept of substituted behavior leads us to another characteristic of the station of disregard. Beneath the calm exterior of acceptance sits a core that is permeated with hostility and resentment. The disregarding mate is like a volcano. The surface may be peaceful enough, but there is no mistaking the force that rests with the molten lava only a short distance away. The actual overt display of this hostility is only occasionally tapped. It far more frequently displays itself in the tendency to be disregarding (therefore, the name of this station) and stubborn.

Interestingly, most of what I have described for this station would be strongly denied by the spouse. Denial is another common characteristic of disregard. Sometimes, a spouse may actually be fairly oblivious to the extent of the situation. But usually, the denial is more of an attempt to fool others than to fool self. A disregarding spouse typically understands the marriage and the bargain.

Mates who enter the station of disregard have the greatest potential for keeping their marriage intact without accomplishing any true and healthy change in the relationship. This is due to the strong bargaining characteristic. As long as the context continues to be stable, then things will be okay. As long as the money is there, or comfort continues, or status is uninterrupted, then the relationship is tolerable. But if the bargain is broken, then problems may appear.

A marriage in the station of disregard is seldom seen for counseling. Though there is dissatisfaction, it has been accepted. The exception to this is found when the bargain is broken. I remember counseling with one couple who had been married for over thirty years. During this time, Kent and Karla had raised two children, both of whom were college graduates with families of their own. Kent had spent his adult life in industrial sales which had proven to be quite lucrative.

The last twenty years had been with the same company. What supposedly brought them to counseling was Karla's dissatisfaction with Kent's "selfish insensitivity."

As we began to discuss their marital history, it became apparent that there was some truth to Karla's accusations. Kent did tend to be somewhat insensitive. But this was something that had occurred throughout the duration of their marriage. The question in my mind was: Why now? Why was Kent's insensitivity, after more than thirty years of marriage, suddenly a significant enough problem to warrant professional intervention? What else had happened?

> We've had a lot of adjustments lately. I've been with the same company for twenty years. Two years ago, they were bought out by another company, and for me to stay with them, I had to relocate. This hasn't proven to be a good move.
>
> My income has dropped from $120,000 to $90,000 and that has brought some financial problems. I can't get Karla to conserve. She just keeps on spending. You'd think we could make it on $90,000. But apparently we can't.

There were some other factors involved in the move. Support groups were lost requiring the establishment of new ones and some longtime hobbies and recreational activities were greatly curtailed with the change in locale. Obviously, there were adjustments to be made with these changes in life style. But these were not the types of problems that healthy individuals with equally healthy relationships couldn't handle. So where was the problem? The problem was with the bargain. It had been broken.

For years, Karla had accepted the disappointing limitations of her marriage. She resigned herself to an unfulfilling emotional relationship as long as she could live comfortably and be free to pursue her own interests. This she could do on $120,000 a year. Kent had placed little restriction on how Karla spent money. With the change in income, however, came an austerity program that infringed on their bargain. And with the bargain broken, Karla again focused on her dissatisfaction with the relationship.

Most marriages encounter external crises and pressures. In healthy relationships these are weathered. In some instances, these experiences actually help to draw spouses closer together, thus creating an even stronger bond of unity. For marriages in the station of disregard, just the opposite occurs. In these relationships, crises serve to push mates even further apart. Like a light shining through the cracks in a piece of broken porcelain, crises only illuminate what is already there. A disregarded marriage may remain intact forever, but only if the bargain also remains unbroken.

Disengagement

The station of disengagement is similar to that of disregard, without the hostility and bargaining. A disengaged spouse has lost hope. He views the relationship as static—as having no chance for change. But for some reason, he has come to grips with this perceived reality and arrived at some degree of peace. It may not be what was desired. And it may not be what is preferred. But "it is what is." And for the spouse, that awareness is not only reality, but also something that is accepted.

What accompanies this acceptance of reality is a decision to move on with a life separate from that of the offending mate: a disengagement. A disengaging spouse lets go of the marriage. There is no more clinging and holding on to what might have been. This may involve a divorce, but not always. Unlike the station of disregard, this decision is not laced with resentment or hostility. The spouse is calm. The decision is simply a final resolve.

To move on separately is foremost a decision regarding control. A disengaging mate comes to the realization that he cannot control the behavior of his mate. Nor would he choose to if he could. But just as clear as the decision to not control, is the resolve to not be controlled either. The irresponsible decisions of an offending mate will no longer be allowed to unduly influence his life.

A disengaging spouse acts instead of reacts. A spouse who "reacts" is either rebelling against the desires or behaviors of a mate or giving in to them. A spouse who "acts," however, considers what would be the healthy and best decision. Once determined, it is enacted. Decisions are not based on spite, resistance, or any attempt at manipulated gain. Instead, a decision is made because it seems best for the individual.

There is an air of selfishness in this station, but that is only because of the context. Due to the loss of hope, it seems only right to the spouse to focus on self-needs to the exclusion of the offending mate.

Of the four stations, this is the healthiest. But as I stressed at the outset, though some stations are better than others, none is good. The station of disengagement, though calmer and more rational than the others, still represents giving up. And as long as a spouse remains in one of these four stations of hopelessness, regardless of the particular posture that is taken, little headway can be made for the marriage.

Final Thoughts

There is a means whereby a marriage that has lost hope can be restored. There is a plan. It may not occur, but the potential is there. The initiation of such a plan, however, will likely rest with the very person who has the least to give—the spouse who has given up.

This is the real danger of the cycle of lost hope—deteriorating to a point where you no longer want to try. It may be that no truly constructive efforts have yet been attempted. Though the marriage has gradually been deteriorating for years, possibly nothing has been done other than passively watching, waiting, and wishing. Regardless of what has or has not been tried, if the relationship is to have an opportunity to resurrect, it will require a decision on the part of the spouse to deal with the marriage. And a decision of this magnitude will probably require more strength than the spouse possesses.

5

On the Subject of Hope

There is a plan. There is a means whereby hope—that essential quality for a marriage that anticipates the future: the element whose gradual depletion brings crisis to a relationship—can be restored. But before we explore this plan, we need to gain a fuller and more complete understanding of hope, especially as it relates to Christians.

There is a hope that anticipates the future for the marriage—and there is a hope that trusts in the providence of the Lord Jesus Christ. With a fuller understanding of the subject of hope, we will discover that, while one of these may falter, the other is steadfast. Though one may wane, the other is certain. Regardless of the outcome of the marriage, there is always hope.

There Are No Guarantees

Stan and Linda had been separated for two years. They came to me for counseling in the hope that they might reconcile their estranged relationship. After several sessions, however, they appeared to be no closer to reuniting than when they first came in. Stan claimed that Linda had never prioritized him in their marriage. He felt that he had always fallen in line somewhere behind the church and Linda's family. It was Stan's assertion that, unless Linda was willing to make him first in her life, he was not willing to reconcile.

Linda's perspective of their relationship was somewhat different. She described her role as being a constant giver. For over fifteen years, her willingness to be totally giving had been the only reason there had been any peace at all within their marriage. In fact, Linda questioned whether she, or anyone else for that matter, could ever give enough to satisfy Stan. Any attempts at independent activity or anything which might detract from what Stan thought should be happening, had been quickly challenged. Therefore, it was Linda's assertion that, unless Stan's demanding and overpowering nature were to change, she was also unwilling to reconcile their marriage.

Though there is a sense that all marriages are cooperative ventures with each mate able to lay claim to both some of the good and some of the bad which takes place, there are those relationships where this distribution is not necessarily equal. Stan and Linda had one of these marriages. Though Linda was probably a little rigid in some respects, this was not the problem in their marriage. "Holding her ground" was more a sign of health than resistance. Had she not finally taken a stand, Stan would have absorbed her entire life. He was that demanding. But this was an assessment that he strongly resisted.

With their positions so firmly entrenched, I decided to see them individually for a few sessions and look more thoroughly at some of their personal issues. It was during one of these sessions that Linda made the following comments.

Stan and I have had some interesting conversations since

beginning counseling. He has admitted to me that he is
extremely resistant to change. He really likes being the way
he is. And he really finds coming to see you uncomfortable.

Stan's resistance and discomfort was not surprising. His coming
to counseling had been the result of an ultimatum from Linda.
"Either come with me to counseling or I'm filing for a divorce."
Linda had left Stan two years earlier because of his involvement in
an affair and his refusal to end it. Though the extramarital relationship
finally dissolved, Stan had made no effort to reconcile his marriage.
In fact, he was even a little angry with Linda for having left him. Stan
now maintained weekly visits with Linda and the children, but for
all intents and purposes, he seemed quite comfortable with their
separation. It was Linda's dissatisfaction that prompted counseling.
Though Stan was not yet ready to return home, neither was he ready
for a divorce. Choosing counseling as the "lesser of two evils," Stan
sought to pacify Linda by coming.

> Stan has refused to go to counseling for years. It is almost
> like he's content for things to go on as they are. I felt that it
> might help to talk to a professional. I've done everything else
> there is to do. I've prayed and prayed—but nothing has
> changed.
>
> This is our last chance. I'm ready for something to
> happen. I don't think I can hold on much longer.
>
> I have felt as though I have needed to do everything that
> is possible for me to do. *But I also realize that there are no
> guarantees. The Lord is not going to force Stan to do anything.
> Stan will have to make his own choices.* I have gotten him to
> counseling but the next step is up to Stan. No one can make
> him change.

I knew what needed to happen for there to be the opportunity for reconciliation. But I did not know whether Stan would make the changes. In the midst of the chaos, Linda had the same understanding. She was going to do all that she knew to do—but she realized that there were no guarantees that even this would save her marriage. And she was not placing the responsibility for the necessary changes on anyone else—not me, not her, and not God. The responsibility was Stan's.

Linda was viewing the situation very accurately—both from an emotional relationships viewpoint and also theologically. She knew *who* was responsible for *what*. Though she greatly desired for things to work out for her and Stan, Linda recognized that there were no guarantees when it came to someone's behavior—that we are all free to choose and act in any manner that we desire.

By taking such a position, Linda was resisting the temptation to bargain with God. It is not unusual for me to counsel with couples who strive very diligently to make sense out of the chaos which they are experiencing. In their attempt at understanding, they frequently ascribe to the Lord more responsibility—both for the creation of their situation and any solution to their problem—than He is due. For example, it is common for me to hear the following comments:

> God does not like divorce so surely He is going to intervene in this situation (whether this intervention means He will bring a mate who has left a marriage home, or that He will cause an alcoholic mate to stop drinking, or . . .);

and

> The Lord is causing this problem for some ultimate good. There must be a purpose. He has to have a reason for this tragedy.

I can understand the need to make sense out of the chaos—to somehow bring order to the disorder. It is also understandable for people to almost magically cling to the hope that good will triumph—that right will prevail. Though these needs and desires are understandable, I do not believe they are accurate. There may be plans and guidelines whereby, if they are followed, situations can improve. But there are no magical solutions.

Linda recognized this reality. She realized that reconciliation *can* occur, but that it *may* not. Hope could be restored, but it might not. Situations could change, but there are not guarantees that they will. We can have hope for a marriage, but it may not be fulfilled. Not because God does not love us, and not because He does not care, but because that is not the way He works.

We are ultimately responsible for what we do—each and every one of us. Linda realized that we can do all that we know to do, but that we can do no more than that. People are still free to make their own independent choices. As much as she wanted her marriage to reconcile, Linda *could not* force any such decision upon Stan—and she knew that God *would not*. Ultimately, Stan would make his own choices and the consequences would affect both him and Linda.

God Always Has a Future for His People

Tossing and turning
Eyes wide open even
    though my lids are tightly shut.
Longing for escape—for sleep
But it does no good.
Scores and scores of memories
    what ifs and promises all parade
    back and forth before me.

You were my life,
  my love,
my everything. But it
wasn't enough.
You wanted something else.

When you left, though, you took
  my dreams.
Unintentionally, maybe, but they all
  rested with you just the same.
Now I'm having trouble
  trying to develop
a new set of
dreams.
After all, how can I dream,
  when I can't even
  sleep.

Joy © (used with permission)

This poem was written by one of my clients. She was in a great deal of emotional pain at its inception. It is a sad poem—written during an even sadder period in her life. Her husband of ten years had decided that he no longer wanted to be married. Together, Joy and I chronicled some difficult times. She is now at a place where things are less painful. Life is being viewed with more optimism. Though her marriage was not saved, she is once again dreaming, and her new poetry reflects the change.

For me, this poem not only speaks of a specific client's pain, but it also serves as a reminder of what I do. I am a counselor. As such,

I am privileged to share in a great deal of heartache. I use the word "privileged" because I view counseling as a ministry. It is an opportunity to be used of God—to somehow extend the love of Christ to those who are in need of that touch.

Sometimes my intervention helps situations to change. An unstable marriage becomes stable; a marriage in crisis becomes reconciled; a family conflict becomes resolved. But changed circumstances are not always the outcome. Sometimes marriages remain unstable; relationships remain irreconcilable; family conflicts remain unresolved; or, as in the case of our poet, regardless of intent and effort, sometimes a marriage ends. In the midst of either gain or loss, I strive to instill this truth: if being Christian gives us anything, it is the reality of *hope*.

In its fuller sense, there is always hope. Even when situations do not turn out as we would desire, for the Christian, there is hope because there is always Jesus. Hope anticipates. It looks forward to the future. And for the Christian, a hope based on Jesus Christ embraces the belief that *God always has a future for His people*:

- For the newlywed couple, riding high on enthusiasm and optimistic expectations, *God has a future.*

- For the 20-year veterans with a vibrant and healthy marriage, *God has a future.*

- For the drifting couple who suddenly become aware of the distance which has crept into their relationship, *God has a future.*

- For the couple in crisis, *God has a future.*

- And even for the one who has been left to stand alone by a mate who decided that things were hopeless, *God has a future.*

Regardless of where we are in the sequence of marital life, *God has a future for us.*

I do not think that we always make the best choices in life. In fact, some of our choices are pretty poor. Sometimes our erroneous decisions are intentional. We know what we should do, but we do something else anyway. But mostly, our poor choices are less malignant. We want to do the best thing but, caught up in the feeling of the moment, the future consequences of our choices are dimmed and the result is pain.

Although some of us manage to make poor choices more consistently than others, no one is exempt. We all have regrets. None of us *always* makes the best decision. Still, regardless of the choices of the past and the circumstances of the present, *God always has a future for us.*

I do not totally understand the "all things" verses:

> And we know that *all things* work together for good to them that love God, to them who are called to his purpose
>
> Romans 8:28

and

> Giving thanks always for *all things* unto God and the Father in the name of our Lord Jesus Christ
>
> Ephesians 5:20

but I believe them. With God, there is always hope—always a future.

Depending upon the choices we have made, as well as those made by some of the people around us, God's future for us may not be what He would have planned earlier in our lives. These decisions may have added a few twists, turns, and detours. And these departures from His plan may now necessitate greater adjustment and effort on our part. Still, *God has a future for us.*

In the next section of this book, we will be looking at God's plan for the return of hope to a marriage. However, in the midst of all of our well intended efforts, we need to recognize where our real hope rests. Whether doing all that we know to do results in our moving in to the marriage or on with life, *God always has a future for his people*, and **a future with God is always good**.

Final Thoughts

There is a plan. Hope can be restored. It may not, but it can. If hope is to have the potential for restoration, however, it will likely require the initiation of the one who has the least to give—the one who has given up. There is no guarantee that doing all that we know to do will result in a restored marriage. But regardless of the outcome, there is still hope.

Though our hope in the marriage may be dashed, our hope in Jesus remains undaunted. We have the fuller hope. There is no guarantee of changed circumstances or of an improved situation, but there is always hope in God's presence.

II

Restoring Hope

6

It Can't Be the Way It Was

Throughout the text of this book, I have referred to the Lord's plan for the return of hope to a marriage. I have asserted that there is a method—there is a means whereby hope can be restored. I strongly believe this assertion. However, it would be difficult to cite a specific scriptural text to support such a claim.

What would not be as difficult a task would be to cite biblical examples of reconciliation—incidences of healing which have taken place within relationships. These seem to be plentiful. It could be argued that reconciliation and the return of hope to a marriage are not the same thing. To this I would wholeheartedly agree. However, the point which I believe to be of paramount importance is this: Though the process of reconciliation and the return of hope are two different and distinct entities, one is found within the other. **The possibility for the return of hope to a marriage is found *within* the Lord's plan for reconciliation.**

For hope to return to a marriage, a spouse will have to witness "change." There will have to be a reason to believe that the future will be different from the past. Within the process of reconciliation, the essential characteristic required for the rebirth of hope—change—is demonstrated. The evidence of change, as genuine reconciliation is approached, then prompts hope's return to a marriage where previously, it has been all but lost.

Much of the remainder of this book will be devoted to a thorough understanding of the Lord's design for genuine reconciliation. But our goal in examining the process, and evaluating whether all of the prerequisites are truly being accomplished, will be with an eye toward the restoration of hope. We will address the need for a mate's "coming to himself" and admission of wrongdoing. We will define remorse and seek to identify why it is essential to the reconciliation process. We will give thorough attention to what change is and what it is not. And because of the special nature of the marital relationship, we will explore the need for a full commitment as the final step for reconciliation.

Each of these steps is essential if genuine reconciliation is to take place. I have summarized these elements with four brief statements.

> "I'm wrong."
> "I'm sorry."
> "I'm changed."
> "I'm committed."

But again, though they are essential elements in the reconciliation process, the added benefit of reconciliation is the rebirth of hope. Through reconciliation—through demonstrated change—the hope for a future that will be different from the past, can return to a marriage.

Setting the Stage

The elements required for the reconciliation of a marriage are clear. But everything has a starting place—a time which you can point to and say, "That is where it began." For reconciliation to occur, and for the return of hope to have an opportunity, someone has to do something to start the process.

Within marriages where hope has been lost, it is frequently the mate who is ready to give up who has to also begin the process for change. It is the mate who is in despair, defeat, disregard, or disengagement who has to take control. Please note that I am not using the phrase "to take control" in the same manner as others might. I am not suggesting that someone be dominated or unduly coerced into any actions. That would be inappropriate. What I mean by control is that people need to take charge of their own lives. Though spouses should not seek to control their mates, neither should they be controlled by them. However, they are responsible for taking control of themselves. Taking responsibility for your own actions is what is meant by "taking control."

If you are in a marriage where hope is either lost or in the process of being lost, you need to take control of yourself. By taking control of yourself—by assuming responsibility for your behavior—you will also be taking control of your situation. Rather than being merely a responder, you will become an initiator. This initiation will begin the reconciliation process. At least, it will begin the *potential* for reconciliation.

There are three steps which you can take that will mark the beginning for change. You must: 1) know what you don't want; 2) know what you do want; and 3) deal with your mate. Accomplishing these steps will not only commence the possibility for reconciliation, but also the return of hope.

Know what you *don't* want

Succinctly, what you don't want is the marriage as it has been. You do not want a relationship marked by a recurring pattern of inappropriate behavior. Whether this identified behavior defiantly attacks the safety and security of your relationship, or in a less malignant fashion, simply blocks or undermines the potential for growth, it has to stop.

What we are referring to here involves *recognition*. You have to recognize what it is that you do not like. But more than recognition alone, we are addressing the issue of *resolve*. You may have been upset with the events in your marriage, and the heartache which these behaviors have inflicted, for years. Yet, there has been little constructive effort on your part to bring about change. Now, you are ready for change.

You know what is no longer acceptable. You can define it. You can describe it. You can give multiple examples of how it has operated in your marriage. And you can articulate the toll it has taken on your love for your mate. But more than that, you are now resolutely ready for it to change.

Know what you *do* want

Whenever I conduct a marriage seminar or retreat, I begin the weekend with a session devoted to describing what *ought* to be happening in Christian marriages. During this session, I give the participant couples the opportunity to state their beliefs. As a group, we discuss each suggestion, making sure that we clearly understand what is being presented and whether or not it is legitimate.

Most groups do fairly well at suggesting what ought to be taking place in marriage. Their lists usually include items such as the following:

- honesty
- predictability
- accountability
- good communication
- safety
- an opportunity to state your needs
- security
- companionship
- a willingness to share in responsibilities
- a willingness to deal with dissatisfactions
- a willingness to talk and share
- a willingness to put yourself out for your mate
- anticipation that your mate will be willing to put himself out for you
- an atmosphere of forgiveness
- a sensitivity to needs
- mutuality in giving
- a sense of respect

This is a pretty good list. And when these characteristics are present in a marriage, there is the strong potential for both growth and stability. But these elements are not present in every marriage. And in those relationships where hope has either been lost or is waning, there are some items from this list that have obviously been missing.

Part of determining what you want in a marriage is found in realizing what is both *healthy* and *legitimate* to expect. As you compare what *ought* to be happening with what is *actually* occurring in your marriage, you begin to determine exactly what you want. You have the right to expect health. You have the right to expect the characteristics which foster growth in a marriage. These are appropriate to expect. Therefore, it is legitimate to want them.

Deal with your mate

There is really no way around this final step. You have recognized what you don't want and you are resolute about your realization. Furthermore, you have determined what you do want and feel your expectations are legitimate. But if the process toward reconciliation is to begin, you will have to deal with your mate. There must be something that brings the desperation of your situation to your mate's consciousness.

This last step is generally not a preferred choice. You fear confrontation; or you rationalize that your efforts will do little good; or you want to wait and let God change your mate; or you claim to no longer care about what happens to your relationship. After all, you have lost hope. But each of these responses represents an avoidance of responsibility. If you are going to take control of your life, you must constructively face your circumstances. That means that you will need to deal with your mate. Here are some suggestions to help you do just that.

State your needs and expectations.

I refer to this as making a *declaration*. It involves stating honestly and directly what you think and how you feel about your marriage. You will want to make sure that your presentation **reflects a caring attitude** for your mate; however, your concern regarding the deterioration of the marriage must also be clearly expressed. You want no doubt of your dissatisfaction.

Identify the behaviors or characteristics that you do not appreciate in your marriage. State what it is that you expect to see changed. Clearly delineate your needs and expectations, as well as the potential consequences if things do not improve. Your mate needs the full picture.

Allow opportunity for change.

The reconciliation process will be articulated in the following chapters. There is no guarantee that your mate will respond in a manner which will lead to healing for your marriage. But whether he does or not, you will need to allow him opportunity to do either. This generally takes time.

Allow the reconciliation process to work, both for healing and for the restoration of hope. Do not respond too quickly. "Test the spirits." However, do be prepared to respond. Again, the following chapters will aid you in determining *when* it is time to do *what*. The overriding theme will be this: you will want to respond when you witness legitimate change in your mate.

Be prepared to stand your ground.

Determining exactly what "standing your ground" may entail will be different for each relationship. Extreme circumstances will call for extreme action. Less extreme situations will warrant less extreme action.

In each relationship, it must be determined what can be lived with and what cannot—what is acceptable and what is intolerable. Relationships where deviancy is the repetitive pattern may call for a separation. The goal would not be for the marriage to end. But sometimes actions as strong as a separation are required if a marriage is to be saved. Once again, extreme conditions call for extreme action.

Whatever your situation, it is important that you thoroughly understand what taking a stand will mean for you. It is equally important that you then be willing to follow through on your resolve. Constructively dealing with your marriage will require some effort. But the results can be greatly rewarding.

The Principles of God and the Power of God

Though I had met with Sarah on several occasions, I had yet to meet her husband. Ken was totally against the idea of counseling. His attitude could be summarized as follows:

> If Sarah wants to waste her time, that's fine. But I'm not going to waste mine. I don't have any problems so there is no need for me to go to counseling.

Sarah's coming to counseling was prompted by concerns about some recent developments in her marriage. She believed Ken had become too involved with a woman he worked with. Though Ken denied anything other than a friendship, Sarah was all too familiar with the signs of something more. During the course of their thirty-year marriage, Sarah knew of three actual affairs. And there had been several other "relationships" that, if not actual affairs, were at least examples of friendships with too much emotional closeness.

I've seen it happen over and over again. It's so predictable. And I know it's happening again. All of the signs are there. Ken's sudden lack of interest in me; his unexplained absences; the reporting of a "friend at work who needs his help"; and unaccounted-for expenditures of money. It's all there.

Of course, Ken denies that anything inappropriate is going on. He's just being a friend. She needs someone to talk to during this difficult time in her life. He's just doing the Christian thing—providing aid in a time of need. "Would you have me stop behaving in a Christian manner?"

He won't stop meeting with her and says that I'm just overreacting. He says the problem is with me and not him. I'm so confused. I know something is going on, but what can I do?

Sarah wrestled with what to do for several weeks. Finally, she decided that she could no longer tolerate what was at best insensitivity and at worst blatant deceit. A visit to her family had been planned for some time and Sarah decided to take advantage of this opportunity to take control of her life. She told Ken that she did not plan to return from her visit. Rather, until he decided to deal with her honestly, break off the friendship, and get professional help for his problem, she would remain with her family.

Ken was furious with Sarah's confrontation. He defined it as an ultimatum and refused to even consider it. Sarah left for her family visit with Ken still upset. As time drew near to when Sarah was originally to return from her family visit, Ken called and asked when she would be coming home. He acted as if nothing had happened—as if Sarah had not been displeased with the relationship nor confronted him with her expectations. Sarah reaffirmed her position. "Until you decide to deal with me honestly, break off the friendship, and get professional help for your problem, I do not plan to return home."

Ken again became furious and ended the conversation by slamming down the receiver.

Two days later, Ken again telephoned Sarah. This time, however, he had a more conciliatory tone. Though he claimed that there was nothing inappropriate with his friendship at work, he would sever contact with this woman. However, he would not agree to seek counseling. He might have a problem with relationships, but if he did, it wasn't anything that the Lord couldn't handle if it were totally surrendered to Him.

> Why do you feel psychologists are the only ones with the answers? We're Christians, aren't we? Before there was psychology, there was Jesus.
>
> There's nothing wrong with me that the power of God can't take care of. Let me deal with it in my own way. Just let this be between me and God.

Sarah did not want to leave Ken. The action was an effort to take control of her life. She could no longer tolerate the relationship as it was. Her leaving, and her expectations, were a part of resolute decision-making. But how could she argue against Ken's assertion that the power of God could deliver him from whatever his problem may be? Sarah called me to discuss the newest development in her struggle toward marital stability and health. I could tell that she wanted to return to Ken and that she found his new spiritual emphasis perplexing. During our conversation, Sarah decided to return to Ken and allow him the opportunity to deal with his problem with the Lord.

As I hung up the phone, I found myself troubled about what I had just heard. But I was unsure why I was perplexed. Part of my confusion may have been that I doubted Ken's sincerity. I believed he had been manipulative throughout his marriage. This could be just another tactic to get things back to the way they were. I also believed that Ken's problem was significant—that it was deeply rooted in his personality. Though I believe in the power of God to heal and deliver, I also know that this is not always His choice. He also uses the skills of professionals for this purpose. Maybe I viewed God's deliverance for Ken as more of a *possibility* than I did a *probability*.

The more I pondered this situation, however, the more it became clear to me that these were not the basis for my perplexity. It was not whether Ken was being honest or not. And it was not whether God could heal or not. It was with the whole issue of God's power. I was concerned about a right understanding between the relationship of God's *principles* to God's *power*. Though Ken was claiming to be reliant upon the power of God, I questioned whether he was violating the principles of God. And if this were the case, was it right?

The principles of God are stated directly through admonitions, and indirectly through illustrations and examples, throughout both the Old and New Testaments. These principles serve as guidelines for the way that we should live. The power of God is how He chooses to intervene in our lives on a daily basis. Sometimes God's power is displayed miraculously through changed circumstances (like healing). At other times, His power is displayed through His presence as we continue to deal with our humanity in less than ideal situations. Still, God's power is always extraordinary. It is beyond us. In pondering how God's principles and power mesh together in a consistent and cohesive manner, I arrived at four conclusions.

Conclusion #1: *God's principles without God's power is at best legalism and at worst humanism.*

Jesus frequently cited examples of those living by the principles of God yet denying the power of God when he described the Pharisees and scribes (see Luke 18:10; Matthew 23:13-37). These men were firmly rooted in the religious establishment of their day. They did all the right things legally, but were not truly godly. There was no place for the presence or power of God in their legalism. Living today by principles alone would make us no less legalistic than doing so two thousand years ago.

True humanists may view my use of the term humanism as actually misuse. However, I can think of no better term for a Christian who lives by principles alone, even if they are God's principles. Without the power of God in our lives, there is nothing left except ourselves. If that's not humanism, then what is? There must be more than principles alone in the life of a Christian.

Conclusion #2: *God's power without God's principles is at best unstable and at worst hysterical emotionalism.*

James referred to the double-minded man as being "unstable in all his ways" (James 1:8). Though James was referring to the person who is unsure of his faith, the same instability is evident in the one who places his trust in emotions alone and discounts the commands of Jesus.

John addressed this issue and said that those who claim to be Christian but do not obey His commands (live by His principles) are liars (1 John 2:3-4). Yet, we are probably all too familiar with those who live this kind of Christian lifestyle. When emotionally up, they are riding high on God's miraculous power. These Christians see God's plan in each of life's events and view Him as willing to meet any need—from prosperity to healing. "All that you have to do is ask." Yet, these same proclaimers of God's power to deliver seem to be so susceptible to human frailty that they continue to live lives inconsistent with godly principles. This form of living is as wrong as those who deny God's power all together in favor of His principles.

Conclusion #3: *God's power never violates God's principles.*

This was the conclusion that bothered me the most about Sarah and Ken. During the remaining chapters of this book, we will thoroughly explore the Lord's principles for the healing of a relationship. This healing is referred to as reconciliation. He has given us these guidelines for living.

Not everyone, however, wants to follow these principles. Responsibilities and principles go hand-in-hand. There is always something that we must do. Sometimes, spouses would prefer that God would just simply change their marriages—that He would reach down and heal the hurt and resentment without their having to deal with each other. I do not believe that this is the way the Lord works. He will not do anything for us that we can do for ourselves. And reconciliation is definitely something that we can do for ourselves. It only requires a willingness to obey His commands.

What Ken was suggesting to Sarah violated the Lord's principles for reconciliation. Where was his genuine recognition of wrongdoing? (As it turned out, there were definitely some wrongs committed.) Where was his remorse? Where was his changed behavior? Where was his commitment to the marriage? **In pleading the power of God, Ken was avoiding the responsibilities inherent in the principles of God.**

Ken's willingness to allow God's power to deal with his life, if genuine, was encouraging. This definitely needed to happen. But it was obvious that this had not yet happened. And if that was going to be the extent of Ken's efforts, then healing would not take place in his marriage. Healing would occur when Ken followed God's principles. The Lord will not bless a relationship that violates these.

Conclusion #4: *The power of God enables us to live by (fulfill) the principles of God.*

Ken desperately needed the power of God in his life. But he needed this power not to *avoid* the principles, but to *fulfill* them. That is true for us all. It is the power of God that allows us to live by the principles of God. We cannot do it on our own.

Ken needed to face himself. He had some deep needs. God's power could give him the strength to do that. Ken needed some healing in his life. God's power would be able to provide that. Ken needed to resist temptation and to live a committed life. God's power could enable Ken to live the kind of life that would be acceptable to Sarah. And Ken needed to walk with Sarah through the principles of reconciliation. God's power would also be sufficient to this task. In short, the power of God could allow Ken to live out the principles of God, but only if he genuinely turned his life over to the Lord's control.

Surrendering his life, complete with its problems, was something that Ken needed to do. He definitely needed to experience both God's presence and power in his life. But doing so would not exempt him from being responsible for his actions. It would not exempt him from walking through the process of reconciliation with Sarah—the admission of "I'm wrong"; the sensing of genuine remorse; the changed behavior; and the renewed commitment to his marriage. Ken would still need to live by the Lord's commands—by His principles. But surrender would bring this goal within his grasp.

Final Thoughts

Ken and Sarah's story brings us to an important point. Most of this book will focus upon the principles of God. Together, we will thoroughly examine the process which has been given to us to bring healing to a relationship. Within this process is found the potential for the resurrection of hope in a marriage. But at no time should we become so focused on the principles that we lose sight of the power of God and His ability to move in the lives of His people.

Paul reminds us of the power of the Lord to work in the lives of His people in his letter to the Christians at Ephesus.

> I pray that your inward eyes may be illumined, so that you may know what is the hope to which he calls you, what the wealth and glory of the share he offers you among his people in their heritage, and *how vast the resources of his power open to us who trust in him.*
>
> Ephesians 1:18-19

"How vast the resources of his power . . ." This should be encouraging to us all. We are to live by the principles of God. But we do not have to do this entirely in our own strength. We have the resources of a loving Father to rely on. There is power in Jesus.

If hope is to return to your marriage, it will come as a result of witnessed change. It will come as a result of the completion of the Lord's principles for reconciliation. The following statements will be made:

> "I'm wrong."
> "I'm sorry."
> "I'm changed."
> "I'm committed."

If hope is to return, it will likely come because of what you do—because you initiated the reconciliation process. But it will also come because of the power of God. **The Lord's power for restoration and healing is displayed when mates have a change of heart.**

7

"I'm wrong."

The first statement an offending mate needs to make is, "I'm wrong." This confession is made in reference to that mate's behavior. Remember, it is the repetitive nature of unacceptable behavior that has caused the hope in the marriage to depart. The first step toward any form of reconciliation, and consequently, any possible return of hope, rests with the mate's honest admission of this wrongdoing.

There is more to the admission of "I'm wrong" than the mere utterance of a few words. It involves a genuine recognition and realization of what has been done on the part of the offender. I particularly like some of the biblical examples of those who learned of their inappropriate behavior.

The scriptural phrase "come to their senses" seems to more truly capture the nature of what is intended by the statement "I'm wrong" than any other that I know. For instance, there is the familiar story of the father and his son, the prodigal (see Luke 15). After pressing his father for his inheritance, and then receiving it, the son set off for a distant country—someplace where the grass would undoubtedly be greener. Scripture records that he squandered away the money and then fell on hard times. In the midst of disappointment, dashed dreams, and the face of stark reality, this prodigal "came to his senses" (v. 17). He recognized that he had been wrong. This realization prompted the following admission.

> The son said, "Father, I have sinned, against God and against you; I am no longer fit to be called your son."
>
> Luke 15:21

My summation of the prodigal's words would be "I was wrong." But as you can tell from the description which we have just witnessed, these words do not come close to treating justly the richness of this passage. "Then he came to his senses" far better captures the true essence of the prodigal's circumstance.

A second illustration of recognized wrongdoing is found with Peter, one of Jesus' disciples. Actually, the verse to which I am referring is Jesus' prophecy that Peter would recognize his own wrongdoing. Jesus was discussing the events that would surround His crucifixion. He included the part where Peter would deny that he even knew Jesus. We will deal more specifically with this event in Chapter 8. However, at this point, what is of primary importance is Jesus' comment to Peter.

> ". . . and when you have *come to yourself*, you must lend strength to your brothers."
>
> Luke 22:32(b)

The term "come to yourself" is a variation of "come to your

senses." But the meaning is similar enough to fall well within the concept of "I'm wrong." Jesus knew what Peter would do—that he would do the wrong thing and that he would fail his Master. But Jesus also knew that Peter would "come to himself." That occurrence would mark the turning point for Peter. Coming to himself would then enable him to move from defeat to triumph.

A final example of "coming to your senses" is found in our key verse in 2 Timothy.

> The Lord may grant them a change of heart and show them the truth, and thus they may *come to their senses* and escape from the devil's snare . . .
>
> 2 Timothy 2:25(b)-26(a)

In this passage, Paul is not speaking of what has occurred. Rather, he is stating what will need to happen if the "refractory" are to escape the grip of the devil. The refractory Paul refers to are those within the church fellowship who may be straying from what is both appropriate and acceptable behavior. Paul admonishes Timothy to deal with them in a manner that may allow them to "come to their senses"—to recognize the error of their ways. Paul hopes that with this realization they would then correct their style of living and resume their fellowship with the Lord and His people.

As we can see, the statement "I'm wrong" has greater significance than is sometimes attributed to it. **This first step toward reconciliation involves an *owning* by the offender of his wrongdoing.** The key elements of "I'm wrong" are: 1) recognition and realization; 2) genuine acceptance and ownership; and 3) admission and confession. If these are present, then the journey toward reconciliation can begin.

Sometimes Recognition Requires
a Little Assistance

My first meeting with Richard had been arranged by his wife. Alice and I had met for one previous session. In great detail, she had related the history of their relationship which included a whirlwind courtship, a rocky eighteen-month marriage, and a painful four-week separation. Now, I was actually sitting down with Richard.

Alice had provided me with a lot of information about Richard. Though I would need to verify the accuracy of what she had shared, there were already some preconceived notions and questions formulating in my mind. For instance, at the early age of twenty-six, why was Richard contemplating the end of his third marriage? Why had he been unfaithful in each of his previous relationships? Did he really have the drinking problem Alice described? Was he a workaholic? And was his resistance to expectations and limitations placed on his behavior as strong as Alice claimed?

I found Richard to be extremely outgoing. He was probably very adept at making good first impressions—the type of person who never meets a stranger. After the preliminary introductions, Richard spontaneously launched into an explanation for his willingness to meet with me, as well as a defense of who he was as a person.

> I'm here because Alice asked me to come. I care about Alice so I'm willing to do anything to help her out. I'm not really interested in the marriage—and I guess I'm not really "in love" with Alice either, but neither do I want her to be hurt.
>
> I actually feel pretty good about who I am. I think I'm a pretty okay person—fairly healthy. I don't think I have any personal problems and I think you'll find the same thing.

> Alice wants me to come back home. I'm willing to do
> that but she'll have to stop putting all of these restrictions on
> me. If she can abide by that, then fine. If not, then we might
> as well end the marriage right now.

Richard was already giving me information that contradicted what Alice had reported. First of all, Alice had said that Richard approached her about reconciling their marriage. He supposedly said that he was not ready for their marriage to end and that he really wanted to come home. In fact, he was insistent on their getting back together as soon as possible. That would be quite a different attitude from the one that Richard presented at our session.

Alice had also indicated that Richard had been sharing with her his concern that he may have some significant personal problems. This too was quite a bit different from the self description which Richard so willingly volunteered in the first moments of our conversation. Which was accurate? Was Richard willing to return to Alice out of the goodness of his heart and in order to "help her out," or did he really desire to return for other reasons? And did Richard really think he was as problem-free as he reported to me?

Our session continued as Richard told me some more about himself. Richard gave me a brief history of his life; some of the significant events in his childhood; the relationship he had had with his parents; his perspective on his two previous marriages and their demises; and his assessment of his current relationship with Alice. The more that Richard talked, the more apparent it became that he was a deeply troubled young man.

At the very best, it could be said that Richard had lived a colorful life. At the very worst, his life could be described as one that had been impacted in the early years by painful events, followed by the resolve on his part to run from both the deeply harbored *old* pain from his past, as well as, every person or situation which might possibly inflict any *new* pain in his present existence.

Richard had been hurt deeply. And his solution for this wound, rather than to let it heal, was to cover it up and to protect himself from any possibility of further hurt. This extreme form of protectionism came at a high cost to Richard, both personally and relationally. In order to feel good, Richard found himself periodically abusing alcohol and throwing himself into his work. He even threw himself into relationships—but only as a taker. When it came to giving, the relationship became too demanding for him. And when the potential for hurt surfaced, Richard simply moved to another relationship.

When we finished the session, Richard asked me what I thought of him. Did I agree with his assessment that he was a fairly healthy person? I told Richard that it was a little early for me to make that kind of judgment, but that he and I might not totally agree on everything. I then asked Richard to complete some psychological tests that would aid me in giving him a clearer answer to his question. Richard consented because, once again, he was willing to do anything that might prove helpful for Alice.

At our next session, it was the same friendly and outgoing Richard who had met with me a week earlier who showed up for the appointment. He acted as if he didn't have a care in the world. Richard wanted to get quickly to the test results suggesting that some of the questions were strange and difficult for him to answer. Prompted by the results of the tests, I asked Richard a few more questions before responding to his inquiries. There had been several problem areas suggested in Richard's test results. I spent some time explaining these findings. Then, I began to deal fairly frankly with him.

Richard, I'm concerned about your life. I hear you telling me that you are happy and that you don't think that you have any problems. But what you're saying and thinking do not line up with what you're doing. *Your beliefs are not consistent with the facts.*

The test results suggest that there are several problem areas in your personality. Through your own admission, there are traumatic events that occurred years ago that you cannot even talk about today without becoming extremely upset. You abuse alcohol and are also a workaholic. At age twenty-six, you have already been married three times and in each of these relationships, you have been unfaithful. Now, you may want to believe that you have no personal problems, but what you are doing is not normal behavior. It is not healthy to live the way you have been living.

Richard, you can choose to continue to believe that everything is okay, that you have no problems, that you are normal and healthy. But those beliefs do not line up with the facts. And as long as you choose to live your life in this manner, and to continue in your misbeliefs, there will be no opportunity for change.

Until you face the facts and honestly deal with your life, you will continue in the path that you have been following for several years. And my concern is that this path will do nothing but cause you even greater heartache than you have experienced already. The choice is yours. What do you want to do? Do you want to continue living in denial? Or do you want to face reality?

Richard held his response for a few moments. When he finally spoke, his jovial façade was replaced with a more solemn countenance. Richard did not make a full admission to really needing some help, but he did admit that there were some areas in his life which warranted attention. Since I primarily counsel with clearly defined marital difficulties, and Richard had some problems of a very individual nature, I referred him to a clinical psychologist who could help him deal with his life.

The point of Richard's story is this: Richard had significant personal problems. But for many years, he had been successfully denying these problems. **Incongruity between what we either say or believe to be true about ourselves, and what is *really* true, is denial.** Sometimes denial is used intentionally. We know that what we are saying is inaccurate, but it is our intent to *mislead others*. But at other times, the difference between what is believed and what is real may not be recognized. In these instances, denial serves to *fool ourselves*.

The apostle John encountered the same incongruity with some who claimed to be Christians. His test for distinguishing between what was true and what was not true, is very straightforward.

> Here is the message we heard from him and pass on to you: that God is light, and in him there is no darkness at all. If we claim to be sharing in his life while we walk in the dark, our words and our lives are a lie; . . .
>
> Here is the test by which we can make sure that we know him: do we keep his commands? The man who says, "I know him," while he disobeys his commands, is a liar and a stranger to the truth.
>
> 1 John 1:5-6; 2:3-4

John's test is simple. Either your claims and your actions are congruent, or you are a liar. Either you are following the commands of Jesus, or you are not. And if you are not, then you cannot claim to be Christian. I did not call Richard a liar. Had I used John's formula, I probably could have. Richard's claims were obviously incongruent with his actions. However, John could just as easily have said that the Christians he was referring to were walking in denial.

How much of Richard's denial was known, and how much was unknown, is difficult to say. From the standpoint of how you treat incongruity, however, it actually makes very little difference. Denial, or incongruity between what is claimed or believed and what is real, is always confronted with facts. That is what I did with Richard. He claimed to be healthy, but the facts (his behavior) were inconsistent with that claim. So I articulated the differences for Richard's benefit.

I confronted Richard with the facts, not to degrade him, but in the hope that he might "come to his senses." Sometimes, offending mates need a little assistance in recognizing that their behavior has been inappropriate. Pointing out the facts—illustrating the difference between what is said or believed and what is done—can aid in a mate's recognition of wrongdoing. When dealing with a therapeutic situation, I call this maneuver "poking holes" in a client's denial system. If a client can be forced to face reality, he then has the opportunity to deal with his life. He may be helped with coming to the personal realization "I'm wrong."

Richard represents a fairly serious example of an individual in a state of denial. There are many ordinary situations which also illustrate this same principle. I once met with a wife whose twenty-year marriage was more than satisfactory until her husband decided to switch careers. He had pastored for over fifteen years but, after several difficult assignments, decided to leave the formal ministry and pursue a career in business. The particular field which he chose to enter became quite demanding of his time which began to take its toll on the marriage. When Megan came to my office, it followed three years of what she described as marital deterioration. She was quite depressed with the whole situation.

> We don't really have a relationship anymore. Dave comes
> in late and leaves early. We have no sex life. We seldom talk
> about anything other than the essentials for keeping the
> house running smoothly—paying the bills and meeting the
> children's demanding schedules. Since Dave left the ministry,
> we don't even talk about anything spiritual. If I try to bring
> up something spiritual for consideration, Dave simply ignores
> me. We never spend time together, either just the two of us
> or with other couples.
>
> No wonder I feel like a stranger. I don't know Dave
> anymore. And what hurts so much is that I don't even know
> if he cares. I don't know what to do. I just feel so bad.

Dave came to see me with great reluctance. He was visibly put
out with the entire situation. True, Dave did have to take time away
from his busy schedule in order to keep the appointment. But the
real resistance came from his basic belief regarding his marriage.

> I think things are okay. They could be better, but they're
> pretty stable just the way they are. There's nothing that a
> little more free time wouldn't take care of.

Interestingly, Dave did not contradict any of the events and
circumstances that Megan had shared the week earlier. The only
difference was the *meaning* ascribed to the events. Megan saw their
situation as desperate and floundering; Dave saw it as stable. My
interpretation was closer to Megan's than Dave's. I saw their
relationship teetering on the brink of a real crisis. Somehow, Dave
needed to realize this, too. Toward the end of the session, I offered
the following observation.

> You know, Dave, I think there is so much distance in
> your marriage that I could drive a truck between you and
> Megan.

Dave appeared a little shocked by my statement. Then he responded with a rejection. He did not agree with me. We had already discussed the six dimensions of intimacy in marriage. Recognizing the absence of these in Dave's relationship with Megan, I stated the facts.

> You and Megan do not have a *sex life*. You do not *talk* about anything that isn't superficial. You never deal with *spiritual* issues and you never spend any *time* together. That makes you zero-for-four. Do you want to try for six?

Dave sat silently in his chair for a few moments. He didn't like what I had said, but neither could he refute it. After all, I had stated the facts.

> You made your point. Maybe there are some things that Megan and I need to deal with. Since you put it like that, I guess there is less stability in my marriage than I thought. It's easy to lose sensitivity.

Dave and Megan ended up counseling with me for several months. During that time, some important changes were made in how they prioritized their time and invested in their marriage. This resulted in a significant improvement in their relationship.

Dave was not a deeply troubled man. He was not a person with significant personality difficulties. In fact, he was just the opposite. Dave was ordinary. But being ordinary had not exempted him from having difficulties in his marriage. Neither had it exempted him from living with denial. When an individual says and believes one thing, yet demonstrates through his behavior something different, I confront him with the facts. This enabled Dave to recognize his error.

The facts broke through Dave's denial. This allowed him to realize that he had been genuinely wrong. By acknowledging "I'm wrong," Dave was able to begin the change process. With the acceptance of "I'm wrong" Dave saved his marriage.

The Goal of Confrontation

Does having a change of heart effect our recognition of the truth, our "coming to our senses?" Or does our recognition of truth, breaking through the denial and coming to our senses, prompt a change of heart? Probably, there are instances where both have happened. But I suspect that the sequence more frequently resembles the second pattern. More likely we, like Paul on the road to Damascus, will first have to "see the light" before other changes can take place.

Sometimes people see the light and come to themselves on their own with little or no assistance from others. They just suddenly have an "Aha!" experience. This is not typically the case, however, especially when you are dealing with long-term, repetitive patterns of behavior. In these situations, lives more often have to come to some form of crisis point before there is recognition. Like Peter, Paul, and many other notables for God who first had to bottom out before being usable, some mates will need assistance in coming to the end of themselves. When offering this assistance—when pointing out the facts in an attempt to poke holes in a mate's denial—there are three factors which are important to bear in mind.

It is not your goal to bring hurt

When dealing with an offending mate, remember *why* you are doing *what* you are doing. Your goal is not to be vindictive or spiteful. You are not seeking to intentionally do harm. Rather, you are seeking to offer opportunity for correction. The full text of our key verse in 2 Timothy expresses the non-vindictive flavor of our stating of the facts. Again, Paul was not speaking specifically of husbands and wives. But his words have implication for all relationships.

> He should be a good teacher, tolerant, and *gentle when discipline is needed for the refractory*. The Lord may grant them a change of heart and show them the truth, and thus they may come to their senses and escape from the devil's snare, in which they have been caught and held at his will.
>
> 2 Timothy 2:25-26

Note Paul's emphasis on "gentle" and "discipline." The meanings of these terms are far from words like "harsh," "vindictive," or "punishing." The point is clear. Our goal is the potential change of the other person and not in the expression of our own pent-up feelings.

When dealing with an offending mate, your goal is to help and not to harm. Bear this in mind as you share the facts.

Not everyone will want to hear the facts

Jesus was good at stating the facts—at dealing honestly and directly with people, regardless of their social or political status. A good example of this is found in a passage from Luke's gospel describing Jesus' return to Nazareth where He had been raised, and His Sabbath day attendance at the local synagogue. Here Jesus took the opportunity to read a prophetic passage from Isaiah regarding the coming of the Messiah. Upon completion of the reading, Jesus stated the facts.

> He began to speak: "Today," he said, "in your very hearing this text has come true."
>
> Luke 4:21

What followed was not pleasant. The members of the local synagogue did not fall at Jesus' feet and worship Him. Nor did they stand and shout praises to God the Father. They stood and shouted, all right, but in opposition and not support. As Luke continues to recount:

> At these words the whole congregation were infuriated. They leapt up, threw him out of the town, and took him to the brow of the hill on which it was built, meaning to hurl him over the edge. But he walked through them all, and went away.
>
> Luke 4:28-30

People do not always want to hear the facts. Whether it be the facts about Jesus, or the facts regarding their own inappropriate behavior, truth is not always well received. If you are dealing with a mate who is in denial, recognize this possibility before you act. Sometimes confrontation is met with an openness and acceptance which results in "I'm wrong." At other times, however, the result may be continued denial, outright rejection, or even, as in the case of Jesus and the congregation at the synagogue, heated anger. Still, you are not responsible for whether recognition and acceptance of wrongdoing takes place. Your only responsibility is in stating the facts. You then allow adults to be responsible for their own choices.

You have to be willing to upset some people

Though it is not your goal to harm a mate, sometimes that will be the result. Even those who ultimately accept the reality that they have been wrong will not enjoy hearing about their shortcomings. Still, regardless of what people may or may not want to hear, and regardless of how they may or may not respond, it is your responsibility to state the facts. Doing so will require a willingness to upset some hearers—not as a goal, but as a very possible reality.

Paul faced the dilemma of whether to honestly challenge denial to help people, or to protect their feelings by withholding the facts of their inappropriate behavior. How he resolved this dilemma, and his feelings regarding the whole issue, are recorded for us in his second letter to the Christians in the church at Corinth.

> Even if I did wound you by the letter I sent, I do not now regret it. I may have been sorry for it when I saw that the letter had caused you pain, even if only for a time; but now I am happy, not that your feelings were wounded but that the wound led to a change of heart.
>
> 2 Corinthians 7:8-9

It was not Paul's goal to cause pain. In fact, doing so caused him more than just a little personal discomfort. But it was a discomfort that he was more than willing to endure for the ultimate potential of genuinely changed hearts.

If you are going to constructively deal with your marriage, it will require a resolve as strong as Paul's. You will need to be willing to state the facts and potentially hurt your mate—not as a goal, but as an inevitable part of being honest and responsible. Hopefully, the results will be worth the efforts.

Final Thoughts

For hope to return in a marriage where it has departed, a spouse has to see change. Movement must be made toward genuine reconciliation. The first step in this process is the realization by the offender that his behavior has been wrong.

This realization of wrongdoing may come from out of the blue. It may be what is known as an "Aha!" experience. With long-term, repetitive behaviors, however, recognition will more likely be the result of some form of confrontation. Somehow, denial will have to be broken; misbeliefs challenged with facts; a crisis precipitated; or . . . Something tangible will probably have to occur before a mate will truly come to his senses.

Regardless of the circumstances, it is important to realize that "I'm wrong" is an essential first step. Its presence alone will not bring reconciliation or the return of hope. But its absence will definitely prevent it. So, assess your situation. Have you heard "I'm wrong?"

8

"I'm sorry."

Tim and Susan were supposed to come together to our first counseling appointment, but a conflict in Susan's schedule prevented her from attending. Tim was interested enough in seeing that the counseling process got underway that he came in by himself. In fact, as he stated it to me, he actually "preferred it that way." Being alone gave him an opportunity to state all of his concerns. There would be less chance of his holding anything back if Susan were not present for the first meeting.

> I love my wife but there are some things that aren't right in our relationship. I guess you'd say we have a communication problem. There are some things that we just can't talk about.

Tim was a businessman who presented himself with confidence and assurance. There was nothing flashy about Tim—just stable. Emotionally, he was somewhat of a "flat-liner." I surmised he would have few emotional highs or lows. He would mostly stay on the same wavelength: cool, calm, collected, and little affected by the people and events around him.

Tim shared some of his and Susan's marital history which gave me a flavor for the significant events in their lives. I did not yet have a sense for the meanings which may have been ascribed to these events, but I was at least aware of their occurrence. Since Tim presented "communication difficulties" as his reason for seeking counseling, I asked him to elaborate on what he meant by "things we just can't talk about" and how exactly he and Susan went about not talking about them.

> We can't talk about her degree. Susan has been going to school for the past four years working on her doctorate. I'm pretty sure she has finished. But I've never seen the degree. Whenever I ask her about it, she just gets upset.
>
> We can't talk about her going to work. Since she spent all that time and energy getting an advanced education, I figure she ought to consider going back to work. But whenever I bring up the topic, she gets upset and says, "You are only interested in me for the money I can earn."
>
> We can't talk about my business. I bought a business here because the economy was not good in the area of the country where we had spent most of our lives. It was a tough decision but I didn't see any better choices. That was two years ago. Yet, whenever something about the business comes up, we seem to get into an argument.
>
> I don't know what's going on. I just know I want things to be different. One of these issues will come up, there will be an eruption, then we'll avoid each other for a few days. We sort of let everything die down and then go on as if nothing ever happened. Everything is fine until the next eruption.

The last few years have been difficult for both of us. But I'm ready for things to be different.

Tim appeared to be genuinely concerned about his marriage and properly motivated to deal with its difficulties. Since I had met with Tim for an individual session, I wanted to meet independently with Susan before we all met together.

Susan was pleasant and cordial, but she was not nearly as at ease as Tim. She reported much of the same history but was less matter-of-fact about the move to Nashville.

> It came at a bad time for me. I was in the middle of a doctoral program and moving away from campus made completing the degree more difficult.
>
> I liked my home, my friends, and my community. It was hard for me to leave everything that was familiar to come to a place where everything would be new and different. To make matters worse, I don't feel as though I had any say in the decision. All of a sudden, Tim just announced that we were moving to Nashville.

Susan went on to explain that she was finally beginning to settle in to her new environment. At long last, they had moved into a house that was satisfactory; the children liked their schools; and they had found a church home. But it still was not a move that she would have preferred to have made.

> Tim and I have very different personalities. To be as smart as he is in so many different ways, he can be so stupid in others. Tim doesn't seem to have emotions and he definitely doesn't understand them in me. That has been a frustration of mine for years.

As we continued to talk, some flesh seemed to form on the skeletal description of the marriage which she and Tim had given me. Since Tim had reported their "communication problem," I asked Susan about it. I even asked about her degree and whether this was as sensitive an issue as Tim suggested.

> Yes, I got my degree. But I put it in a drawer. I've never shown it to Tim and I don't know when, or even if, I will. He doesn't deserve to see it!

Susan's last statement was made with intensity. She obviously had some strong emotions towards this issue but was surprised when I made the observation that she seemed angry with Tim.

> Angry? Well, I haven't given that much thought. But maybe I am angry with Tim. He certainly deserves it if I am.

After meeting with both Tim and Susan individually, I began to see them together and to address the reasons why they came to counseling: their lack of communication and Susan's anger with Tim. It took a few sessions, but finally, a rationale for their difficulties began to emerge. Their relationship had operated for years with a *distancer-pursuer* dynamic. In this form of a relationship, one mate (frequently the husband, but not always) finds emotional closeness to be uncomfortable. As a result of this discomfort, he generally places most of his attention and energies outside of the marriage. The other mate, who desires closeness, finds herself drawn into a role of frequently asking for something that her mate would prefer not to give. This makes for a difficult relationship over the course of the marriage.

Tim clearly appeared to me to be an emotional distancer. For him, this was a natural and automatic emotional posture. Tim invested in things other than the marriage, such as his career. Emotional activities, like sharing his feelings or listening to Susan's, represented foreign needs to him and were largely uncomfortable. He was most at ease when dealing with tangibles. Tim was truly a "just the facts ma'am" kind of man.

Susan needed more than just the functional aspects of a marriage. Therefore, she had been frustrated with the lack of emotional development in their relationship for most of the years of their marriage. The move from their long-time home only exacerbated an already tense situation. If progress were to be made in their marriage, we would have to change the distancer-pursuer dynamic which dictated how they interacted with each other.

This hypothesis seemed plausible enough to Tim and Susan, so we embarked on a treatment plan. What followed was several months of resistance. Counseling appointments were frequently canceled and rescheduled (we met nine times in five months); suggested readings were not completed; assigned tasks were put off to the last possible moment and, on the occasions when they were completed, they were said to be "stupid"; and any serious discussions attempted by Tim and Susan deteriorated into fights. In short, we were getting nowhere.

As I pondered Tim and Susan's situation, the lack of progress became glaringly apparent. I decided to confront them and see what, if anything, we could do differently. To my surprise, Tim and Susan had reached the same conclusion. In a spontaneous statement, Tim summarized his and Susan's perspective on their problem.

> We're not getting anywhere in counseling. I think I know why. I don't think Susan likes me very much. And I know I resent her. I think it goes back to the events surrounding our move to Nashville over two years ago. We're both still mad about what happened then.

Susan agreed with Tim. That was the first consensus I had seen between them on any issue in five months of counseling. The more we talked, the more apparent it became that their assessment was accurate. I had missed it. My description of their relationship was correct. They had a distancer-pursuer dynamic operating in their marriage and it needed to be changed. But that wasn't the current problem. Before they would be ready to work on that aspect of their marriage, they would first have to resolve the resentment that was created in their relationship two years earlier. But were they ready to do that? I didn't think so.

I believed they were still polarized—still stuck in their own positions of justification. Tim and Susan were still focused on how they had been wronged—on their own hurt. They would have to see their own wrongs, and the pain that their behavior inflicted on their mate, before they would be ready to let go of the past. So I sent them home with a task.

> You're right. The real issue that frustrates your marriage right now occurred two years ago. That whole encounter has left you both bitter.
>
> I think I know what it will take to resolve the problem. There will have to be some forgiveness—both sought and extended. You will both have to sincerely ask for *forgiveness* and you will both have to willingly be *forgiving*.
>
> I know what it will take. I just don't know if you can do it. I definitely don't think that you are *ready* to do it now. So I want you to go home and get mad at each other. You've been avoiding the real issue for years. Talk about what was done and how it hurt. Tell each other about your pain. I'll see you in two weeks and we'll see if you are ready to let all of this resentment go.

That prescription was not a suggestion that I typically give to clients. But I felt it would be helpful in this situation. Things were already beginning to get better. I had seen more emotion in Tim in that session than I thought possible. There actually appeared to be some emotional life in this flat-liner.

I didn't exactly know what to expect when Tim and Susan returned to my office. They reported an absolutely miserable two weeks. They had taken my assignment seriously, venting much of their pain from the incident that had for two years been a heavy companion to their marriage. I began by addressing the pain that had been mutually inflicted.

To Susan:

- "Tell Tim what he did that hurt you so much two years ago."
- "Tell Tim how that made you feel."
- "Tell Tim what it made you think—of how it caused you to doubt his love for you."

To Tim:

- "Did you realize this? Did you realize that you were causing Susan all this pain?"
- "How does that make you feel now?"
- "If you had it all to do over again, what would you do differently?"

• • •

To Tim:

- "Tell Susan what she did that hurt you so much two years ago."
- "Tell Susan how that made you feel."
- "Tell Susan what it made you think—how it caused you to doubt her love for you."

To Susan:

- "Did you realize this? Did you realize that you were causing Tim all this pain?"
- "How does that make you feel now?"
- "If you had it all to do over again, what would you do differently?"

As Tim and Susan worked through this sequence of honest sharing, they began to clearly see the pain they inflicted on each other. And when they saw this pain, and what they had done, it caused them even more pain. This new pain, however, was not for what had been done to them. Rather, it was for what they themselves had done to each other. "How does what you did make you feel now?" This new pain was *remorse* for their own inappropriate behavior.

In this particular situation, Tim and Susan each needed to feel remorse before they would be in a position to truly reconcile their relationship and let go of the past. Susan had been crying since halfway into the session. But by the close of the session, Tim, the flat-liner, had joined his wife with tears. They were both expressing remorse. Each was spontaneously saying "I'm sorry." Each was voluntarily asking for forgiveness. And each was just as voluntarily extending it. A genuine reconciliation was achieved that night. The harbored resentment was resolved. Tim and Susan were each able to let go of their particular perception of the past. And all of this was possible because of remorse.

I continued to counsel with Tim and Susan a while. After all, there was still the distancer-pursuer dynamic in their marriage to be addressed. But now they were ready to face it. The resistance was gone. Appointments were kept; reading assignments were completed;

tasks were no longer stupid; and conversations did not erupt into verbal fights. Some adjustments were still needed, but now Tim and Susan were both cooperating toward the same goal. Genuine remorse had allowed their marriage to turn a corner.

A Change of Heart

The second statement needing to be heard from an offending mate is "I'm sorry." I believe that what best captures this quality in our key verse from 2 Timothy is the phrase "a change of heart."

> The Lord may grant them *a change of heart* and show them the truth, and then they may come to their senses and escape the devil's snare . . .
>
> 2 Timothy 2:25(b)-26(a)

Whereas, "I'm wrong" represents the cognitive element in the reconciliation process, "I'm sorry" represents the emotional. "I'm sorry" sounds simple enough. Yet, its meaning is so deep. The Psalmist David frequently spoke of being "broken" before the Lord.

> The sacrifices of God are a broken spirit,
> A broken and a contrite heart—
> These, O God, you will not despise.
>
> Psalm 51:17 NKJV

The terms "broken" and "contrite" do much to clarify meaning. "I'm sorry" is not meant to be glibly spoken. What we are referring to is sorrow—deep emotion which emerges from brokenness.

Genuine remorse is the sorrow that springs from a recognition of the pain which is caused to another. That is what Tim and Susan both experienced. Their genuine sorrow for the pain that each caused in their marriage prompted their tears. It was their sorrow—their remorse—that allowed their relationship to be reconciled.

A good New Testament example of remorse is Peter. We are all familiar with Peter—Peter the apostle, Peter the impetuous disciple, Peter the man's man, the rugged fisherman, Peter the rock, and Peter the denier, the one who denied Christ, not once but three times.

Peter's rapid descent from one who would give his life for the Master to one who denied he even knew this person called Jesus, is recorded in each of the four Gospel accounts. The disciples had just completed what would be their last meal with the Master. It had been an intimate time of sharing between Jesus and those He had poured His life into. After singing Passover hymns, they journeyed to the Mount of Olives (see Matthew 26:30-35). Then Jesus informed His disciples that they would all "fall from your faith on my account." Peter's responses to what had to be a shocking revelation from Jesus, as well as a more crushing prophetic statement, are recorded below.

> Peter replied, "Everyone else may fall away on your account, but I never will."
>
> Jesus said to him, "I tell you, tonight before the cock crows you will disown me three times."
>
> Peter said, "Even if I must die with you, I will never disown you."
>
> Matthew 26: 33-35(a)

At the garden of Gethsemane, Jesus was apprehended and led off to the house of Caiaphas the High Priest. Though the rest of His followers fled, Peter followed at a distance and remained outside in the courtyard while the guards mocked, beat, and spat upon Jesus. It is interesting to note that the first person to confront Peter was a serving maid. In fact, Matthew uses the term "accosted." I have difficulty picturing Peter, the rock and the fisherman, being accosted by a serving maid. But that is what happened. This was like rubbing salt into a wound. And when accused of being a friend of Jesus, Peter's response was, "I do not know what you mean" (v. 70).

The second accuser was also a girl. Peter's response was similar, though somewhat more vehement. This time, with an oath, Peter said, "I do not know the man" (v. 72). The third and final accusation came from bystanders to which Peter again responded, with curses and another oath, "I do not know the man" (v. 74). With the third denial, prophecy was fulfilled and "a cock crowed."

Peter had completed his descent. And he knew it. John records that the cock crowed, but says nothing more (John 18:27). Luke takes us a step further and points out that Peter "remembered the Lord's words" regarding the denial and the cock crowing (Luke 22:61). Though Mark records Peter's emotional response to his failure, "And he burst into tears" (Mark 14:72), it is Matthew who shares the *depth* of Peter's emotion: "He went outside and wept bitterly" (Matthew 26:75).

Peter had not died for his Master. He could not even admit to knowing Him. The crowing cock might just as well have been a professional prizefighter taking practice on Peter's skull. The realization of what Peter had done struck him a severe blow. Peter was devastated. He was defeated. He knew he had failed his Lord. And he was in great sorrow.

Peter's genuine remorse prepared him for reconciliation. Sometimes our situations seem to get worse before they get better. I imagine that things looked pretty dismal for the disciples. First, Jesus was arrested. Then He was crucified. To make matters worse, His body had disappeared. Was it stolen or was He alive? Things were in a chaotic state. What do you do when things are chaotic? Well, Peter went fishing. John records the events like this.

> Simon Peter said, "I am going out fishing."
>
> "We will go with you," said the others.
>
> So they started and got into the boat. But that night they caught nothing. Morning came, and there stood Jesus on the beach, but the disciples did not know that it was Jesus. He called out to them, "Friends, have you caught anything?"
>
> They answered, "No."
>
> He said, "Shoot the net to starboard, and you will make a catch."
>
> They did so, and found they could not haul the net aboard, there were so many fish in it. Then the disciple whom Jesus loved said to Peter, "It is the Lord!" When Simon Peter heard that, he wrapped his coat about him (for they had stripped) and plunged into the sea. The rest of them came on in the boat, towing the net full of fish; for they were not far from land, only about a hundred yards.
>
> John 21:3-8

What a day. What an opportunity. What a change in circumstances. Peter could not wait to see the Lord. Once he learned that it was Jesus standing on the shore ("It is the Lord!"), he immediately plunged into the sea and headed for Him. The rest of those who were fishing came in a more conventional manner. They came by boat. But that was not fast enough for Peter. He had to get to the Master— and he had to do it quickly. There were things that needed to be said.

We can only imagine what that initial conversation was like. It is not recorded in the Gospel accounts. But with a remorseful Peter, and a forgiving Lord, my guess is that reconciliation took place. The necessary ingredients were present.

To Seek Forgiveness

Tim and Susan, the psalmist David, Peter the apostle—what do all of these have in common? They have all experienced forgiveness. And they have all experienced forgiveness that was preceded by remorse. There was a genuine sorrow that sprang from the recognition of their inappropriate acts. And this sorrow cleared the path for reconciliation.

Forgiveness *is not* based on a mate's behavior. He may continue to behave inappropriately, never truly realizing his errancy and never experiencing remorse or regret for his acts. Still, he can be (indeed, he must be) forgiven. Though forgiveness is not dependent upon the behavior of a mate, reconciliation *is*. We can continue to forgive. We can continue to care. But the restoration of hope—hope for things to be different, after multiple problems—is based on a genuine change of heart. It is not enough to say "I'm wrong." This admission must be followed by a genuine statement of "I am also sorry."

When I first met with Larry and Diane, it became quickly apparent that hurt had been inflicted by both partners in this relationship. But is was also apparent that only one of them was truly willing to own any responsibility for wrongdoing. Larry openly acknowledged his part in their difficulty and for this he was remorseful. Diane, on the other hand, was tenaciously clinging to the hurt which Larry had caused her. She would admit to not being perfect. But in her mind, there was no comparison between her behavior and the terrible pain which Larry had put her through. Though Larry was sorry for his behavior, it angered him that Diane would not forgive him, nor would she accept responsibility for her behavior. They seemed to be caught in a stalemate.

I asked that they go home and mentally swap places. I wanted Diane to imagine how she would have felt if she had been treated in the same manner in which she had treated Larry.

> What would you think? Would you think that you were loved? Would you think that you counted for anything in the relationship—that you were prioritized?
>
> How would you feel if you were treated in this manner? Would you feel good? Or would you feel bad—hurt, disappointed, angry?
>
> And what would you do? Would you be loving? Would you withdraw? Or would you attack in some manner? Give this some thought.

Several schedule conflicts prevented our getting together again for about a month. But the change in Diane and the relationship itself was noticeable from the outset of the session. Diane's intensity was gone. In its place was a solemn countenance. I asked how they were doing. Diane answered.

> I think we're doing better—a whole lot better. Over the past few weeks it has really hit me just how much I hurt Larry. I didn't mean to do it—but I did. And I'm so sorry for it.

Tears were streaming from Diane's eyes as she continued to speak. She talked about specific things that she had done—some with intent, but many without. And as she spoke and shared her sorrow, the anger that Larry had been storing towards Diane's failure to own her responsibility in their marital deterioration, slowly slipped away. Genuine remorse worked a miracle in their marriage that night.

Final Thoughts

The examples which we have examined in this chapter underscore the importance of saying "I'm sorry." There can be no reconciliation without these words. They are more than easy utterances. They represent a deep emotional sorrow. Remorse is a realization that someone has been hurt because of something you did. And this realization causes the offender some pain. There is regret.

Emotions are not something to be worked up. They are either present or they are not. When evaluating this characteristic in the reconciliation process, one theme needs to be embedded in your understanding. **To seek forgiveness, without genuine remorse, is to not seek forgiveness at all.** Without remorse, there will not be reconciliation. And without remorse, hope will not return.

9

"I'm changed."

The third statement needing to be heard from an offending mate is "I'm changed." This statement refers to the inappropriate behavior which has repeatedly been a part of the marriage. After all, it was the repetitive nature of this behavior that led to the loss of hope. It is unrealistic to expect hope to return as long as the behavior is present.

Any realistic anticipation for the resurrection of hope in a marriage must be preceded by a significant change in behavior. Though behavioral change is observable, this is a more complicated issue than you might think. For example, how do you know when the desired change is "for real?" How do you know that the desired change will last? And how do you know when the change that has been evidenced is enough?

These are difficult questions. And to some extent, there may not be any way to answer them absolutely. Though there are no guarantees when it comes to assessing change, there are some factors which can clarify your situation. As you try to evaluate whether or not the change has reached an acceptable level, the following considerations will help provide you with a sense that you are either moving in the right direction or further work is still warranted.

Considerations

As with the other reconciling statements, "I'm changed" carries with it certain demonstrations. To help us sort through the complexity which encompasses the entire issue of behavioral change, I have posed the primary considerations in the form of questions. Work through the questions and see how your relationship is faring.

Has the change in behavior been *preceded* by: 1) a coming to senses, and 2) a change of heart?

My talking to Darryl was more of a casual "catching-up" with the events in his life than it was a counseling session. I had counseled with Darryl and Trudy for a short period of time but it had been over a year since I had seen them. In fact, the last information that I had received indicated that they were separated with Darryl living in another state and Trudy contemplating a divorce.

> Things were pretty rough there for a while. But you won't believe how they've been the past six months. It's been great. Our marriage has never been this good. There are some things that we probably need to work on, but Trudy's being as kind to me and I'm being as kind to her as either of us could hope for.

Those were surprising words. Darryl and Trudy had come to me for counseling some time earlier because of the extreme hostility that each was demonstrating in the marriage. They were tired of fighting. Both desired peace but they did not know how to achieve it. As we delved into their marital history, it became apparent that this argumentative problem was not an episode but a life style. They could be aptly described as "weary warriors."

Counseling had produced little change in their situation. Though they would try to behave in a more acceptable manner, any change would only be short-lived. Attempts on my part to address any contribution that one or the other might have to the deterioration of the relationship was dismissed. They continued to be polarized or pushed to extremes, each believing that it was the other who was at fault and in need of change. This resistance to change was complicated by their attitudes. Each felt clearly justified in clinging to their position.

Counseling seemed to get them nowhere. Scheduling conflicts arose and except for an occasional telephone call from Trudy, we lost touch. It was Trudy who had told me of the separation and possible divorce. But that was over a year earlier. I wondered what had happened to change things for them.

> I went to California with no intention of returning. I needed the peace. There was a good job waiting for me and, since Trudy and I couldn't manage to do anything but argue, it seemed like an easy out.
>
> We had very little contact for the first month or so. Then I began to think about our marriage and how I had really treated her. For the first time during the twenty-five years of our marriage, it began to hit me that I hadn't been a very good husband. I hadn't been very giving. And when I did do what Trudy wanted, I was always "standing up on the inside." I saw her requests and needs as demands—and I know she could sense my rebellious attitude.
>
> Don't get me wrong. I'm not saying that Trudy was

spotless in this whole thing. But I truly saw my own part in
it. I began to pray that the Lord would deal with my heart
and help me to be the husband Trudy deserved. That's when
I decided to return. It's been good ever since.

What Darryl was sharing made perfect sense. Prior to this
revelation, he did not really want to change. He wanted Trudy to
change how she treated him, and he wanted his marriage to be
different, but he did not really want to change anything that he did.
Though he might attempt to do things differently, there was always
an air of resistance accompanying the efforts. And changes were
made begrudgingly. Even the admission of wrong was misleading.
Darryl used the "yes, but" technique. He gave lip service to having
done something inappropriately, but the real problem was always
with something Trudy had said or done. With the "yes, but" technique,
the admission is only a camouflage for what the person really
believes. The truth is found in everything that follows the "but" in
the statement.

Darryl was saying that, prior to the separation, he had never
really come to his senses, truly embracing his own wrongdoing, and
he had not felt genuine remorse for how this behavior had affected
Trudy. This made his attempts at change futile. Now, with both of
these steps accomplished, he was ready to seriously change some of
the areas in his life that had been errant for years. The sustained
change had definite positive ramifications on his marriage.

The real difference is found in the "want to." At least, that is how
another client phrased it. He, too, had been in a marriage with a
history of conflict. When this couple's marriage finally approached
a point of crisis, they came to counseling. Much like Darryl and
Trudy, this couple too seemed to bog down in accusations and
resentment. I saw them for quite a while and the relationship got

worse before it got better. But gradually, there seemed to be a change. What precipitated the turn for this couple? This is how the husband stated it to me.

Things are different now. When we first started coming, you probably had to erase my heel marks from the carpet in your waiting room. I was here because Marti demanded it. I was determined to continue to do and be as I had always done and been.

Gradually, I did start to cooperate. However, even when I did start to do some things differently, it was with the attitude: "Listen, I'm doing better. What more do you want?" Anything that I did was with resistance. There was always a hint of hostility. After all, I was being forced to do something that I did not want to do.

The real change came when I recognized that Marti was right. She did deserve more from me than she was getting. I did have a problem with being emotionally closed—with not sharing. I did need to change. This realization did not automatically make me any more emotionally open. But it did make me "want to" deal with that area of my life and our marriage.

I no longer resent her needs. Things are different now because I want to work on the problems. I want to change.

These two situations illustrate the importance of mates truthfully making the statements "I'm wrong" and "I'm sorry" before they proceed to "I'm changed." Without this progression the longevity of any perceived change in behavior can be severely questioned.

Has the change been *demonstrated* over a period of time?

"I'm changed" seems to be a straightforward and simple enough phrase without eliciting much confusion. Yet, like many other issues that appear to be easily understood, "I'm changed" seems to offer some perplexity. Generally, the confusion centers around the interpretation which is given to the word "change." What is meant by "I'm changed?" What *meaning* do you give to this phrase?

Confusion rests with the various tenses of the verb "change." Is the meaning based on the *past* tense form of the verb, its *present* tense, or its *future* tense? Differentiating between these three forms is helpful as we determine whether there has actually been a change in behavior. We will find that, though these words are easily spoken, what someone means by "I'm changed" may not be real change at all.

"I'm changed."

This is the past-tense form of "change" and represents the "demonstrated reality of a changed behavior." The meaning is clear. The way a spouse is known to behave is in the past. He has changed. The old behavior has been replaced by a new behavior. He is now different from the way he used to be.

Any time that "change" is used in this past-tense form, there ought to be a visible and noticeable difference in behavior. That is why I used the word "demonstrated" in the definition above. If something has changed, you ought to be able to see the difference. If a mate who has tended to be irresponsible throughout the marriage has changed that behavior, this will be demonstrated by more responsible actions on his part. And if a mate who has tended to be selfish and controlling has changed those behaviors, this will be seen in his actions that are more giving and more flexible than before.

In short, the past-tense use of "change" means: "what was is no more." Things are different. And the proof of this statement is clearly observable.

"I'm changing."

This is the present-tense form of the verb "change" and represents the "demonstrated reality of a behavior that is in the *process* of changing." One of the key elements to the meaning of this form of "change" is the recognizable difference between the way things used to be and the way they currently are. This emphasis on a demonstrated difference is something which the present-tense meaning holds in common with the past-tense meaning of "change". A significant difference between these two tenses, however, is the lack of finality associated with anything "in process."

"I'm changed" has a clear-cut sound to it. The implication is arrival—being finished. Whatever needed to happen has been completed. There is no such connotation with a term indicating that a process is in operation. Rather, what you see today may be different from what you saw yesterday, but it is also different from what you will see tomorrow. With process, you have not yet arrived. Further change can be anticipated.

If a mate who has previously tended to avoid dealing with any dissatisfaction in his marriage is *changing* that behavior, this will be demonstrated by more direct actions on his part. He may not yet be good at dealing with conflict. But he will be better—and he will be concentrating on enhancing even this improved level of achievement.

In short, the present-tense use of "change" means: "what was is no more and, though there is a difference, I'm still not through." Things are different, but they are still in process. There will be further changes.

"I will change."

This is the future-tense form of the verb "change" and represents the "anticipation of a future change of behavior." The key distinction between the meaning of "change" in the future-tense and the two meanings which we have just examined is the lack of any demonstrated change in behavior. To state "I will change" is to *promise* to change while having not yet done so. Change has not occurred and there is no evidence or proof that it ever will. There is only the stated intent.

There is not much that can be said about this form of "I'm changed." If an abusive mate "will change" sometime in the future, what does this mean for the marriage now? And if a mate who is addicted to some chemical substance "will get help" for his addiction in the future, what does this mean for his problem and its effect on the marriage today?

In short, the future-tense form of the word "change" means: "What was still is but I'll change sometime in the future." There is no evidence of behavioral change.

Acceptable meanings of "change"

When someone says "I'm changed," what exactly does he mean? Many people can speak the same words and have totally different meanings and intentions. From the perspective of an offended spouse—one who has spent years with a mate whose repeated display of inappropriate behavior has drained the hope from the marriage—there are certain meanings of this phrase that are acceptable, and there is one that is not.

Remember, there must be a demonstrated change in the behavior of the offending mate and this change needs to have been evidenced for a substantial period of time. Using this as a guide, you are interested in behavior that has either been *changed* or behavior that is *changing*, but not behavior that *will change*. You cannot accept the promise of change of inappropriate behavior. You cannot accept the promise of change alone.

If a mate has changed from his former behavior, or is in the process of changing, and then offers promises of even greater change for the future, this is quite acceptable. In fact, it may even be desirable. But the promise of change alone—the promise of something for the future without the willingness to do anything different in the present—is totally unacceptable. This meaning of "I'm changed" is usually only a ploy. The likelihood of the mate following through on the stated promise is small.

Assess your situation. What have you observed? This will give you understanding of what is meant by "I'm changed." Be sure you can live with the meaning.

What is the *goal* of the change?

As Carol sat in my office, she was a classic illustration of defeat. With a gaze toward my bookcase, it was obvious from the look in her eyes that she was tired. Carol was not scanning for any particular titles. She was just staring. Her eyes were as expressionless as the rest of her countenance.

I had first seen Carol several months earlier. Her mood was somewhat different then—more a case of despair than defeat. She was depressed, anxious, not sleeping, and not eating. She had lost hope in her marriage of ten years and saw no way out. She felt trapped. Allen had spent most of those ten years unemployed. He claimed that he wanted to work but he just couldn't find the right job—a position for which he was ideally suited. Over the years, what began as a supposed case of bad luck gradually took on the distinct flavor of blatant irresponsibility.

Carol grew weary of being the primary breadwinner in the family. Without the help of friends and family, there were times when she, Allen and their three children would not have had enough to eat. Allen's irresponsibility went further than his unwillingness to be employed. He contributed little effort at home either. His primary activity was operating the remote control for the television. Finally, Carol had had enough. "I can raise three children, but I refuse to raise four." It was at that point that they came to counseling, though our contact was very limited.

Carol and Allen's relationship was at a real point of crisis. Allen was aware of Carol's displeasure but was not willing to make any changes. After a short period of time, Carol asked him to leave the family until he could contribute to it in a meaningful and responsible manner. Reluctantly, Allen moved in with his parents.

For several months, things remained virtually unchanged. Allen kept asking Carol if he could come back home but he made no efforts to find employment. He lived off his parents just like he had lived off Carol. His request to return was consistently denied. Though there was no change in the situation, Carol's countenance had improved. Allen's absence from her life alone seemed to reduce at least one source of stress. Her depression subsided and some degree of stability returned to her personality.

Finally, some changes began to occur. Allen found a job and, for the first time in over three years, started to bring home a paycheck. He even began helping Carol out at home by watching the children in the evening so she could run errands. Allen never stopped pressing Carol to let him move home, but at least things were more promising.

After a month of his employment, Carol gave in to Allen's pressure. After all, Allen had changed the area of primary complaint—his irresponsibility. With his new job and his willingness to help out at home, Carol was sensing renewed hope for their future.

That was three months ago. And now, once again, Carol was in my office. This time she was in defeat. And I anticipated that despair might not be far away. Why the change? What precipitated her return to see me? Slowly and methodically, with little expression, Carol answered my questions.

> Allen "lost" his job—again. Really, it's more like he quit. I've been through this so many times. I really thought he had changed. I guess I was wrong.
>
> Things looked so hopeful while Allen was living with his parents. But when I said he could come home, it was the "old" Allen, and not the new, who returned. He stopped helping around the house and began complaining about his job. He didn't like the work; he didn't like the boss; the boss didn't like him; the pay wasn't any good. . . . I've heard it all before. Two weeks later, Allen began laying out "sick," showing up late, and leaving early. A week later, they let him go.
>
> I can't really blame his boss. They need someone they can depend upon. So do I.

Carol paused. "I don't know what to do." Carol was defeated—and understandably so. It is bad enough to lose hope in a marriage. It is worse to have the flicker of hope, gone and then revived, abruptly blown out once again. There are several things that Carol could have done differently. She could have waited longer before allowing Allen to return home. This would have given him more opportunity to demonstrate change. She could have required counseling to help Allen come to his senses. With Allen's history, these would have been very reasonable expectations. But she didn't. The result was devastating.

Carol seriously misjudged Allen. She accurately assessed a change in his behavior—but she misperceived his intent. Although Carol had hoped that Allen had genuinely faced himself—recognized his need to change and set as his goal the decision to take responsibility for his life—his true goal had actually been to simply get back home. With this accomplished—with his goal reached—Allen then returned to his former behavior.

Rather than to change, sometimes a mate's goal is "to *not* change." Mates who cling to this goal will do whatever it takes in order to get things back to the way they were. Regardless of the wishes and needs of others, and regardless of what is either healthy or unhealthy, right or wrong, they just want things to be normal again. For Allen, this meant his getting a job and cooperating with some of the household responsibilities. But this was a change that he only had to demonstrate until the situation returned to its previous state. Then it was business as usual.

What is the *goal* of the change? This is not always easy to assess. Unless it is the result of serious recognition of the need to change and a real desire to take responsibility for this need, the change is not likely to be legitimate. If the goal is to manipulate, to persuade, to pacify, or to appease, it can be classified as "doing the *right* things for the *wrong* reasons." As such, it is unacceptable.

Has there been any *real* change?

By now, the fallacy of the old adage should be clear: "What you see is what you get." Though we do want to see a change in behavior, what we actually get may be very different from what we see. Judging behavior is never an easy task. We frequently see only the tip of the iceberg. Though the tip is something that definitely must be seen, there is still much that rests below the surface—far from view. What is hidden from view makes the determination of what we are really getting so difficult.

To some extent, this was part of the problem with assessing the *goal* of change in the previous section. Allen's behavior was clearly visible but his goal was far from view. We could only guess that Allen was doing the right thing for the right reason. This problem of uncertainty with what we are really getting plays out in other ways. With some mates, we may see a desired change. **But in some situations, a *great deal* of change must take place before there is any *real* change at all.**

A good illustration of this is the Clarks. Mike and Jeannie came to counseling during a highly intense time in their marriage. Each was extremely hostile. Jeannie was angry about twelve years of emotional and verbal abuse. Throughout the marriage, Mike had been controlling and domineering. It seemed that the more Jeannie did to try and make him happy, the more insensitive he became. The proverbial straw that broke the camel's back for Jeannie was Mike's drinking. Though he drank throughout most of their married life, his bouts with alcohol had increased to such a level that Jeannie found it no longer tolerable.

Jeannie's hostility emanated from her frustration with Mike's flagrant and repetitive display of deviant behavior. Mike's hostility was a response to Jeannie's ultimatum for counseling. Jeannie had given Mike a choice. He could either come with her to counseling or she would leave him. Given those two choices, Mike accompanied Jeannie to counseling. But it infuriated him.

What followed were several non-productive sessions with Jeannie's pleading for safety and security and Mike's denying even the existence of a problem. From his perspective, the only problem was Jeannie's demands and her lack of willingness to be the Christian wife she ought to be. Mike saw nothing that couldn't be improved with simply a little more acceptance and submission on Jeannie's part. Finally, Jeannie left the marriage.

Jeannie's departure really incensed Mike. He was initially belligerent. But his threats failed to persuade Jeannie to return. With the apparent failure of force, Mike turned to the tactic of acquiescence. With this approach, he readily admitted to having a problem and promised to get help if only she would return. (Remember our discussion of "I will change.") Jeannie held firm to her decision. She would not return home unless Mike demonstrated distinctly changed behavior. Ultimately, Mike admitted himself into an alcohol treatment program. After a month of intensive treatment, he was released and labeled "substance free." He was no longer drinking and vowed to remain sober.

Mike's first telephone call after being discharged was to Jeannie. He explained his conquering of the alcoholism that had controlled his life, and asked her to come home. But Jeannie was not ready for that step. She told Mike that she was happy for his success, but she needed a little more time and space before she would feel comfortable enough to return. "Just give me a little more time." And what was Mike's response to Jeannie's request? He was livid.

> What do you mean you want "a little more time?" We've already been separated for three months. I've done what you

wanted. I've gone to treatment. I've stopped my drinking. You need to come home.

You're changing the rules and I don't like it. Our bargain was if I stopped drinking, you'd come home. Well, I stopped. Now, you'd better come home.

Jeannie continued to stand firm on her position of wanting more time. But the longer she waited, the more coercive Mike became. He even threatened to bring Jeannie before their church on charges. "You're violating your Christian responsibilities."

Jeannie was in a quandary. She was confused by Mike's behavior. He had stopped drinking. For that she was thankful. But in many other ways, he was still the same old Mike.

I'm glad for what has happened in Mike's life. But he still acts the way he used to before he stopped drinking. Whenever he doesn't get his way, he gets very upset. I don't think he has *really* changed at all. Mike is his old self—and that scares me to death.

Remember our thesis statement: In some situations, "a *great deal* of change must take place before there is any *real* change at all." This fact is demonstrated by Mike and Jeannie's relationship. When it comes to dealing with addictions, this is not an uncommon problem.

Addictions represent complicated issues. There is always more to the problem than simply abusing a chemical or pursuing an activity. Whatever is being obsessively pursued is visible, but it's only secondary. The real problem rests within the individual and not with his addiction. The following diagram will help explain what I mean.

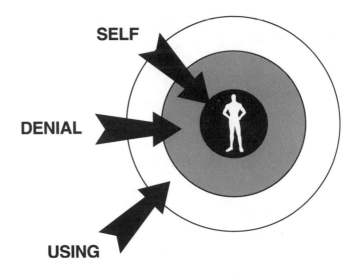

At the center of the diagram (the core) is the self. This is the personality of the individual—who he is, what he believes, how he feels, etc. If he is particularly troubled, experiencing a great deal of pain, or does not like what he sees, he may set up an outer ring of psychological protection. This is denial. By using denial (often beyond his awareness), he is able to hide the pain and dissatisfaction which really exists in his life. With some people, denial is not enough. They then pursue something to offer additional protection— something to help shield their pain. The substance of choice could manifest itself by any number of items—high achievement, relationships, food, and even chemicals. It may be anything that will bring some immediate relief to their pain.

Mike's choice was alcohol. This substance helped him avoid the pain in his life. But the alcohol was not the real problem. It was only the means Mike used to avoid dealing with the real problem—his self. To experience real change, Mike will have to honestly face himself. The core will have to be penetrated. Though he had successfully broken through the outer protective layer of using a medicating substance, Mike was still surrounded by denial. He still protected himself from the belief that there was really anything wrong with him as a person.

The change which Mike had experienced was commendable. It had to happen. But it was the beginning—not the end. Stopping the medicating was a necessary prerequisite to facing himself. But if all the change that was going to take place for Mike was sobriety ("I'm sober"), there was no real change in Mike. He would continue to respond from the core of his life. He would continue to be demanding, controlling and insensitive. Unless Mike takes the next step and breaks through the layer of denial that continues to protect him, he will continue to be "his old self." Mike will have to demonstrate more change for Jeannie to be able to accept any change.

Assessing Change

Is the change "for real?" Will it last? Is the offending mate doing the right things for the right reasons, or does he have other motives? Is there a goal other than honestly desiring to offer more to the marriage? Has there been enough change? These are difficult questions. Hopefully, you are now better prepared to answer them.

There is no way to be totally sure that what you are seeing is what you are actually getting. Assessing behavior is never easy. It involves more than mere observation. Though assessing behavioral change is not easy, neither is it entirely a matter of chance. There are factors to consider. With due deliberation, and reliance upon some basic and sound principles, the level of your assessment can be significantly improved.

10

"I'm committed."

The final statement that needs to be heard from an offending mate is "I'm committed." This statement is made regarding both the marriage as an institution and as a relationship. A full commitment from an offending mate encompasses a willingness to do whatever it takes to insure the continued growth and survival of the marriage. As with the other reconciling statements, there is more to commitment than words alone.

More specifically, what does the statement "I'm committed" mean for the reconciling marriage? When we talk about "doing whatever it takes," what exactly is this referring to? What has to be done? Generally, "I'm committed" means that an offending mate is willing to *deal* with the marital relationship. There is an evidenced willingness to deal with the marriage in its *present* tense—the pain, the tension, the difficult emotions—and there is also a willingness to deal with the marriage in its *past* tense and *future* tense—the particular characteristics which have interfered with the development of a healthy relationship, and which, unless resolved, will continue to do so. In both of these instances, dealing with the marriage will likely require a professional counselor.

Indications

As with the other reconciling statements, "I'm committed" carries with it certain demonstrations. You can measure whether what is being stated is actually true by what is being done. A mate will indicate his willingness to deal with the marriage in two ways: 1) by dealing with the present tense emotions, and 2) by dealing with the past/future characteristics of the relationship.

Dealing with the present

When I first met with Jennifer, she described a marriage that, for the most part, had been characterized by calm and peace. For over ten years, she and Jeff had lived together with very little friction. They did not argue. They did not fight. Instead, they very cordially and cooperatively worked together to see that the demands of daily routines went as smoothly as possible. It became apparent, however, that what Jennifer had contently viewed as tranquil, was in fact far more malignant.

Though Jennifer and Jeff's relationship had had few disruptions, apparently there had also been little to bind them together. Rather than simply peaceful, their relationship could more accurately be described as "drifting." There was no overt and obvious tension. But neither was there any emotional bonding—no in-depth and personal investment being made in the relationship. In a subtle, peaceful drift, Jennifer and Jeff had gradually moved further and further apart.

Drifting marriages are historically crisis-prone. Though they may drift along for an extended period of time, they are being primed for disruption. And this proved to be the case for Jeff and Jennifer. The particular form of disruption which had precipitated a crisis for Jeff and Jennifer was another woman. Jeff had an affair.

When Jeff told me he was leaving, I was stunned. I couldn't believe my ears. Maybe I was a fool, but I didn't have the first clue that there was a problem.

I couldn't understand what was happening and why he wanted to leave. Jeff was reluctant to give me any answers. Finally, he just leveled with me and said he was seeing someone else—that he loved her and wanted to be with her. He couldn't see any reason for staying away from her any longer, so he wanted out.

Nothing has ever hurt me like that moment of disclosure. That was when I lost it. I really fell apart. Jeff moved out and it was all I could do to make it through the day.

I thought the marriage was over so the children and I packed up and moved home with my parents several hundred miles away. I needed to be some place secure. That really helped. I had very little contact with Jeff during this time. He sent me money on a regular basis but we seldom talked. I could have pursued a divorce but I was in no hurry so the situation just kind of rolled on.

After a couple of months, however, I realized that, as supportive as my family had been, my real home was where I had spent the last ten years of my life and not where I had spent the first twenty. I began to really miss my friends and the community. And I also began asking myself: "Why should I let Jeff drive me away from where I want to be?" So I moved back.

That was five months ago. Since then, things have been

gradually changing for Jeff and me. He started dropping by the house just to see how I was doing. Then he told me that his affair was over. Since then, his stops have become more frequent and he even occasionally spends the night. Jeff won't talk about the affair. He only says that he thinks he may be ready to come home.

Well, I'm confused. I love Jeff and I want my marriage to stay together. I wouldn't have given that much chance of happening when he first left. *But I've got questions—and I've got feelings.* What do I do with these? Do I just forget them and let Jeff come back when he's ready? Do we just forget the past? Am I to pretend it never happened? Or, is there something else to be done? What am I to do?

Jennifer was asking some significant questions. The significance was twofold. First, Jennifer was confused. She did not know what to do and her confusion was prompting some anxiety—some personal discomfort. She needed to determine a course of action, to reduce her tension. The second area of significance was of even greater importance than the personal discomfort that accompanies confusion. It involved consequences for her relationship. The course of action decided on would have far-reaching effects on the ultimate healing of her relationship with Jeff.

It is not unusual for an offending mate to prefer to avoid dealing with the questions and feelings of an offended spouse. In fact, avoidance of this type is the preferred choice. Some mates even get obstinate about it.

If you can't forget about what happened and just let it go, then I guess there's no point in my coming back. I'm not going to listen to it for the rest of my life. You're never going to forgive me. You're never going to forget it. You're always

going to bring it up. I can't live that way. So it's in your
hands. Either forget it or forget me.

I am not describing a situation that has been repeatedly resurrected
and thrown into the face of a mate over a long period of time. That
would be inappropriate. Rather, this is the manipulative maneuver
of a mate who does not wish to deal with the present tense of a
marriage—at all.

Offenders frequently would rather pretend that whatever has
taken place never happened. "Let's just start fresh." Even though
there is a sense that the marriage does need to "start fresh," this will
not occur unless the questions and feelings are first faced.

Unanswered questions haunt a marriage. They prevent a spouse
from successfully letting go of the past. And unexpressed feelings
act as an emotional block to a relationship. These unresolved emotions
fester. As with the failure to adequately clean out a fresh wound on
your physical body, the debris which is left from the failure to
resolve deep emotional hurts can cause infection. This infection
interferes with the healing process. Between the haunting of
unanswered questions and the blocking of unexpressed emotions,
the healing of a relationship has little chance. Both of these areas
need to be resolved if a marriage is to progress.

So, what was Jennifer to do? Jeff was giving strong hints that he
was ready to move home and officially resume their marriage. Jennifer
wanted to deal with the present tense of their relationship. Jeff
preferred to pretend that nothing had ever happened. So again, what
was Jennifer to do?

I informed Jennifer that her needs to deal with the relationship
were both legitimate and healthy. To do this, however, would require
Jeff's cooperation. I suggested we schedule a time for Jeff to meet

with me alone in order to evaluate just how committed he really was to this marriage. Was he truly ready to return to the marriage? Was he willing to deal with Jennifer? These would be my questions.

Jeff shared a marital history that fairly paralleled the description given by Jennifer. He had not realized the deficiencies that had existed in his relationship until "the other woman" came into his life. The affair had not been planned or calculated. "It just happened." At any rate, Jeff suddenly found himself emotionally overwhelmed and behaving in a manner that was previously uncharacteristic for him.

> It all seems pretty unbelievable now . . . kind of like a nightmare. I sure wouldn't have pictured something like this happening a year ago.
>
> I guess I just want it to be over with. I'm ready to go home. I just want Jennifer and me to get on with our lives—to put this all behind us.

Jeff appeared sincere regarding his desire to resume the marriage and to move on with his and Jennifer's life together. As we talked, I began to explain the normality of his preferences to forget the past. But I also explained the errancy—the failure to heal followed by the failure to bond.

> I know it's uncomfortable. I know you want to start fresh. I know you want what happened to be forgotten. But that's not reality. You are going to have to face Jennifer and deal with this relationship if you want it to heal.

With some hesitancy, Jeff expressed commitment to his marriage. Real commitment is doing what is in the best interest of the relationship in spite of what may be uncomfortable for you personally. That is what Jeff chose. Avoiding, pretending, forgetting—these were the most comfortable approaches. Dealing, however, was the most committed.

Jeff and Jennifer dealt with the present tense of their marriage. Things got a little intense during the session. But a corner was turned in their relationship. The resolution that came from this very uncomfortable time together allowed for some healing—it laid to rest some ghosts and it defused some strong and blocking emotions. That is what dealing with the relationship "where it is" is all about. Cleaning out the wound and getting rid of ghosts allows letting go of the past. By so doing, Jeff and Jennifer were able to move one step closer to restoration.

Dealing with the past/future

If "pretending" is the term that best summarizes the challenge to the commitment of dealing with the present tense of a relationship, then "naïve" has to be the best term for the challenge to this next indication of commitment. Mates preferring to avoid dealing with the particular characteristics which have historically been a part of their relationship, do so with magical thinking. They optimistically believe that "things will naturally be different." Unfortunately, there is no reason for that belief. At least, there is no valid reason. Why should things be different? There is actually no reason to believe that things will be any different from the way that they have always been.

The characteristics and tendencies of interaction in a marriage are actually present before the vows are exchanged. Marriage changes nothing but the intensity of the developing relationship. It exacerbates what is already there. So if a mate is insensitive before the marriage, he will continue to be insensitive even after the wedding. If a mate is an emotional distancer before the marriage, she will continue to be an emotional distancer even after the wedding. And if a mate avoids conflict before the marriage, he will continue to avoid conflict even after the wedding. Things will continue as they have been unless a couple attempts to adapt the patterns they have been so deeply ingrained into the fiber of their relationship.

In marriages where hope has been lost, it is highly unlikely that any healthy adaptation has taken place. In fact, the lack of any changes probably contributed to the relationship deteriorating to the point of crisis. That being the case, what *was* there is *still* there—and what *is* there *will continue* to be there. That is the past and future I keep referring to. The problems that have been in the marriage will continue to be in the marriage unless they are faced and successfully dealt with by the couple. Doing so will require, and will also be an indication of, commitment.

When I first met with Alisha and Allen, the initial indication of commitment had already been demonstrated. Allen had faced Alisha and allowed her to both ask questions and express feelings. It had been a difficult encounter but one that seemed to relieve a great deal of pressure for them both. Now, Alisha saw the need for further counseling, but Allen, feeling a sense of relief, saw no need for anything other than proceeding with the marriage—as it was.

> I admit we had some problems. But those have all been settled. I'm really glad it all came out. It's been like a breath of fresh air for our marriage. But I'm not sure why we're here now.
>
> Things are good between Alisha and me. There are no secrets. There are no hard feelings. I'm no longer doing what I was doing. So, why the need for counseling?

The behavior that Allen referred to involved a long term deception on his part. He had a hobby involving collecting and restoring old model trains. That was innocent enough. The problem came when Allen found himself spending too much of their non-discretionary money on his hobby. Rather than face Alisha with the situation, Allen obtained a loan to cover some of his debts. One deception led to another. To keep this loan a secret, Allen established a personal mailing address by renting a post office box. A separate checking account and several charge accounts followed, all of which he had mailed to his post office address.

Allen's scheme was elaborate. But he found the keeping of secrets and blatant deception to be warring. Finally, like a house built of cards struck by a strong wind, his well-maintained scheme came crashing down. And with Alisha's awareness of Allen's deception, their marriage entered a crisis.

> Allen's been fine ever since I found out about the financial mess he is in. He was carrying around so much guilt. When he says he's relieved, I believe him. But I have some concerns.
>
> I still don't understand why all this happened. And what's to stop it from happening again. I want to trust Allen but I just need some clarity, or understanding, or something. I don't really know what I need. All I do know is that I'm uncomfortable with where things are.

Allen was thinking naïvely. "Things are fine now. Let's just get on with our marriage." Alisha, however, had some concerns. She was not naïve. She knew that the deception did not just happen. There were reasons for its development. And she knew these needed to be faced.

I asked Allen and Alisha to give me a history of their relationship. It had been congenial enough, but a theme began to emerge. Allen tended to refrain from confrontation. The financial deception that prompted the crisis was a significant incident. But it had been preceded by several other times when he avoided dealing with a subject that might bring reaction from Alisha. Allen had a *pattern* for avoidance—not just an incident.

I was not yet sure of Allen's motivation. The whys are always more difficult to determine than the whats. But the behavioral pattern was clear. As this theme became clearer, the naïveté which had so much been a part of Allen's makeup slowly began to dissolve. Allen would have preferred to avoid this area of his marriage. He recognized that dealing with the characteristic patterns that had interfered with the growth and development of their marriage would not be comfortable. But he was committed to the marriage. And this commitment was demonstrated by his willingness to pursue counseling. With Allen's commitment, changes were made in their marriage, and their relationship began to grow.

Final Thoughts

In *The Drifting Marriage*, I addressed the issue of commitment in marriage. There, I differentiated between marriage as an *institution* and marriage as a *relationship*. I argued that for a marriage to grow, a complete or full commitment was required. There needed to be a commitment to both the marital institution *and* relationship, as opposed to merely one *or* the other.

That entire exegesis was valid, but largely theoretical. After publishing *The Drifting Marriage*, I began to look at the more practical extensions of the theory. More specifically, how exactly do you measure commitment. Measuring commitment to marriage as an institution was easier. That could be derived from divorce statistics. Did a couple remain married or not? Regardless of the quality of the relationship, even those who were miserable could demonstrate commitment to an institution. My real quandary, however, was with marriage as a relationship. How could this be measured in a tangible way?

After I struggled with this question for several months, the answer became clear.

> Commitment to marriage as a relationship is measured by the degree to which a spouse does what is in the best interest of the relationship as opposed to what is the most comfortable personally.

Commitment is indicated by a willingness to do what is right, even though that particular behavior may be uncomfortable.

In situations where mates are attempting to foster the return of hope in their marriages, commitment is evidenced by their willingness to deal with the present and past/future tenses of their marriage. This will not be a comfortable thing to do. Avoidance is the preferred choice. But it is essential that these aspects be faced. Their commitment—their willingness to do what is right instead of what is most comfortable—should be taken as an encouraging sign that hope can be based on something tangible.

III

Living the Hope

11

Facing Forgiveness

With genuine change comes the possibility for the return of hope. It is truly amazing what the combination of coming to senses, a change of heart, true commitment, and changed behavior can mean for the outlook of a marriage. As one of my clients remarked, "Genuine remorse washed away a whole lot of *stuff*."

A sense of relief, however, is not always a spouse's response. And a renewed passion for the offender does not always accompany his changed behavior. Sometimes the pervasive feelings are hesitation, apprehension, or fear. The offending mate has done all of the right things, but the spouse is literally scared to death. Another of my clients aptly summarized this sentiment in a counseling session.

> I don't know what to do. I've been through so much. My head tells me that there might be a chance now. But my feelings are so mixed up.
>
> I'm so confused. But so much of what I've felt and gone through so far has been predictable and normal, I'm probably not the Lone Ranger on this either. Am I?

My client was correct. She wasn't the first spouse to ever deal with mixed emotions. Perplexity at a time like this is probably more the norm than it is the exception. Our mind thinks one thing: It recognizes potential. But our emotions are hesitant: They cling to the past. This presents a dilemma for the spouse who wants to go further in the reconciliation process. This decision will require the successful clearing of several hurdles.

The Deep Hurts

Forgiveness and reconciliation are related elements, but they are different. Sometimes confusing their differences creates a problem. Let me offer a few words of clarification. Forgiveness requires only one person. It is solely an independent act. Reconciliation, on the other hand, is interactive. Two participants are required.

For the Christian, forgiveness is a responsibility. We are told to be forgiving. This is not a burden arbitrarily placed on us by an uncaring Lord. Like everything else we are commanded to do, it is clearly intended for our best interest. There is an old saying: "The people you hate control your life." This means failing to forgive is more damaging for the one harboring the resentment than it is for the one who committed the deed. It is the Lord's desire that His people be free from this kind of encumbrance, therefore, the instruction to forgive.

Forgiveness is singular. It requires only one active participant. Jesus could successfully forgive those who crucified Him, regardless of whether they desired His forgiveness or not.

Father, forgive them; they do not know what they are
doing.

Luke 23:34

Reconciliation, though, is plural. It requires two active participants. This is illustrated in Luke's Gospel with the familiar incident we briefly referred to in Chapter 7, the story of the father and his prodigal son. The son wanted his share of inheritance. His father gave it to him. The son immediately embarked on a journey to a distant country where he squandered his money in reckless living. This lifestyle was a total contradiction of the values he had been raised with. After living this way for a while, subjected to many hardships as a consequence of his behavior, he "came to himself." In essence, he recognized the error of his ways. It was then he decided to return to his father's home and ask forgiveness. Luke takes up the rest of the story for us.

> "I will set off and go to my father, and say to him, 'Father,
> I have sinned, against God and against you; I am no longer
> fit to be called your son; treat me as one of your paid
> servants.'" So he set out for his father's house. But while he
> was still a long way off his father saw him, and his heart
> went out to him. He ran to meet him, flung his arms
> around him, and kissed him. The son said, "Father, I have
> sinned, against God and against you; I am no longer fit to
> be called your son."
>
> But the father said to his servants, "Quick! Fetch a
> robe, my best one, and put it on him; put a ring on his
> finger and shoes on his feet. Bring the fatted calf and kill it,
> and let us have a feast to celebrate the day. For this son of
> mine was dead and has come back to life. He was lost and
> is found."

Luke 15:18-24

The relationship between the father and the son was reconciled. But what allowed this to occur was not the father's willingness to forgive alone. Nor was it the son's genuine remorse and request for forgiveness alone. Reconciliation was possible because both of these aspects were present. There was a genuine *forgiver,* and there was a genuine *forgivee.* With reconciliation achieved, healing in the relationship could begin.

Ultimately, reconciliation and the process for the return of hope come to this point of forgiveness. For the marriage to be truly reconciled, forgiveness will have to be extended by the spouse. At that point the relationship can begin to heal. Without reconciliation—though the marriage may remain intact—the pain and injury will persist, blocking any opportunity for a healthy relationship. Consequently, the Lord's design for marriage will not be attained.

Forgiveness, and therefore, the completion of the process of reconciliation, can be difficult in marriages where hope has been lost. The repetition of offending behavior can cause what one client called a "deep hurt." This type of injury can lead to a *grudge.* Clinging to a grudge—tenaciously holding on to the past—can prevent reconciliation and is a hurdle that must be faced to accomplish the return of hope.

The severity of holding a grudge can be illustrated by two couples I recently counseled. The first was Bob and Rachel. I saw them on only one occasion. Bob's request for a divorce precipitated their contacting me. Rachel broke into tears as she entered my office, and she continued to nervously fidget with her keys throughout the session. She was apparently upset with the current circumstances in her life.

> I don't know what to say or do. I'm in total shock. Bob just walked in and said he wanted a divorce. I didn't see it coming at all.

We had some problems early in our marriage but the last twenty years have been good. At least, I thought they were good. I don't understand what's going on.

Bob sat calmly and patiently while Rachel spoke. He did not appear ruffled by what was being said or by Rachel's obvious distress. In the midst of this emotional chaos, Bob was pleasant, but stoic. When Rachel finished, Bob made a few comments, but offered no real explanation.

It's not my desire to hurt Rachel. I'm concerned about her. We've been married for nearly twenty-five years and she's the mother of my children.

We have had a pretty good marriage, but I feel nothing for Rachel. She and I both deserve better than that. I'm doing this for her good as much as I am for mine. I just want the marriage to end so we can both move on with our lives.

People don't *just* fall out of love. There had to be more to their story than this. Rachel alluded to some problems in their marriage. It was possible these earlier problems might have something to do with the way things were now. But Rachel hesitated to elaborate on this in any specific detail. Rachel wanted to skirt around the early years, but Bob wanted to avoid discussing the marriage entirely. He was here at Rachel's insistence. Bob seemed to prefer that I simply accept his explanation at face value and let them leave my office.

I needed more information—to know more about their marital history. So I decided to press them a little.

You know, this isn't making a whole lot of sense to me yet. There are reasons why things are as they are. Let's try and fill in some of the holes. Tell me about your marriage— from the beginning.

With some hesitancy, the real story began to unfold. And with it, my confusion began to disappear. The first four years of marriage were indeed difficult for both of them. Amidst the early pressures of trying to establish a home (babies and careers), their personality differences began to take effect on the relationship. Bob was a good man, but somewhat emotionally distant. With his new job which often kept him away from home, Rachel began to feel neglected and isolated. She needed more from Bob than the memory of "I love you" spoken immediately after "I do." Though dissatisfied with the marriage, Rachel did not deal directly with Bob. Instead, she suffered in silence. Gradually, she grew resentful toward her husband.

After a few years of being emotionally dissatisfied with her relationship, Rachel had an affair. Actually, she had three affairs in one year. When Bob learned of the affairs, their marriage entered a crisis. For a brief time they were separated. Divorce was contemplated. But the decision was made to preserve the family unit. By this time, they had two children and Bob felt they could at least stay together for their sake.

Rachel had been extremely remorseful about what she had done. In response to Bob's decision to remain in the marriage, Rachel recommitted her life to God and vowed to be true to her husband. Though recommitted to the institution, however, Bob and Rachel never really dealt with either the events precipitating the crisis or the marriage itself. They just resumed living together, picking up where things left off. They put a plastic bandage on what required the skilled hands of a surgeon. Bob had his career and continued to be emotionally distant while Rachel raised the children. The greatest difference was that Rachel also committed herself to being the best wife any man could want. The last twenty years had been marked with stability. There were few arguments. Cooperation was their theme. Everything looked fine, which explained Rachel's complete surprise with Bob's request for a divorce. So what was going on?

When they finally spoke honestly, the source of their problem was traced back to the marital crisis some twenty years earlier. Bob was still holding a grudge.

> I was devastated when I found out about the affairs. I would have been hurt with just one—but three! She might as well have cut out my heart with a knife.
>
> I almost divorced her then. But I cared too much about my sons. So I vowed to myself to stay with Rachel until they were grown. Then I would leave. Well, that time has come. Both of my sons are now on their own, so I want out.

Bob's twenty-year-old resentment began to show through his pleasant exterior. He was still nursing the grudge and now, after years of waiting, was ready to uphold his vow. Bob's response elicited only anger and disgust from Rachel.

> I have spent twenty years trying to make up for what I did. I've given and given. I've been the best mother and wife anyone could ask for. But it hasn't been enough.
>
> I was wrong—but I can't change that. It infuriates me that you still haven't forgiven me. Don't the last twenty years count for anything? Haven't I proven my love and faithfulness?

There was no justification for Rachel's behavior twenty years earlier—nothing that could make it legitimate. No excuse could make it right. But I could understand how it happened. I could see how the marriage was allowed to deteriorate. This deterioration was not Rachel's doing alone. Nor was it entirely Bob's either. Rather, it was a joint effort. The affairs were symptomatic of a faltering marriage. But marital crises can be successfully survived. Crises do not have to cause the death of a relationship. But for Bob and Rachel, the crisis was winning.

Bob and Rachel had held their marriage intact, but they failed to truly reconcile their relationship. That merely postponed the inevitable. Bob carried the wound of that crisis with him for years, taking care to conceal it from view. Rachel knew that things were not perfect, but she was compelled by guilt. She was on a mission of mercy. "If I try hard enough and long enough, I'll make it up to Bob. Everything will turn out all right." They went through the mundane motions of a marriage until finally, Bob was ready to leave.

I would like to say that Bob eventually realized the need to face and resolve his grudge—that he finally let the past go and truly reconciled his relationship with Rachel. But that is not what happened. Bob refused to let the grudge go. He chose to hold on to the hurt, letting go of his marriage instead.

The thoughts of Bob and Rachel were fresh on my mind as I sat with Carl and Lois. The similarities in the two marriages were frightening. The greatest difference was that one was past tense and the other was in the present.

Carl and Lois's marriage had survived a crisis some six months earlier. At least, their relationship was still intact. Carl had confronted Lois regarding an affair nearly a year ago. She first denied the accusation but after unmistakable proof, finally confessed. What followed was far more painful for Carl than learning of the affair itself.

> I confronted Lois with the evidence and she finally confessed. But what really hurt was that she would not stop. She kept assuring me that it was over. But she was only

deceiving me. The affair was still going on. Finally it ended—
but that was after nearly six months of my pleading and her
lying. I just can't let that go.

Lois admitted her deception. This was the first act of unfaithfulness
in their fifteen years of marriage. The marriage had been faltering for
several years but both Carl and Lois chose to avoid the warning
signs. It was easier to avoid reality—to pretend that things were fine—
than it was to face and deal with their relationship. Then along came
the proverbial knight in shining armor.

> I was a fool. I see that now. But I was blind at the time.
> My emotions were so out of control that I didn't care about
> anything or anyone but myself. I didn't care what I did or
> who I hurt.
>
> I'm so ashamed. I've been trying for six months to make
> up for being a fool. But Carl can't get past the hurt. I know I
> hurt him—and I'm so sorry for that. But he's going to have to
> forgive me. I can't continue to live with the coldness and his
> episodes of belligerence.

Carl was holding a grudge. Lois had dealt him a harsh blow—a
truly "deep hurt." As understandable as the pain was, however, the
continued grudge would only serve as a hurdle in the process of
recovery for this marriage. It was something that Carl would either
successfully face and let go of, or it was something that would
destroy his relationship with his wife.

These two illustrations involved deep hurts and grudges
precipitated by affairs. Extramarital involvements are painful
encounters. But grudges can also emerge from what might be perceived
as lesser evils. Remember Donna and David, the avoiding couple in
Chapter 3. Donna also had a problem with holding a grudge.

> I'm angry with the way David has treated me—not on just one occasion, but throughout the history of our marriage. I don't know if I can ever forgive him.

And what was David's response?

> I need a fresh start. I was wrong and I believe I'm making some real headway in changing my life. But I can't keep paying for my past. At some point, Donna is going to have to let it go.

A grudge is a hindrance to the reconciliation process. And it can be tenacious. But there comes a time when, if your mate has truly changed what he can offer to the relationship, and if you are going to move ahead with your marriage, you are going to have to let the deep hurt go. **This may require a power beyond your own.**

Beyond Ourselves

There are principles involved when dealing with forgiveness. For example, when dealing with a couple, I frequently look at the indiscretions on both sides of the relationship. Usually, mates do not wear absolutely white or black hats—mates are neither totally villains nor totally heroes. As a person recognizes his own need for forgiveness, he is generally far more open to extending it as well. With the deep hurts, however, I have found that it is often difficult for mates to live by principles alone.

In times like these human frailty becomes evident. The realization that the power of the Lord extends beyond His principles also becomes clear. If you have trusted the Lord to change your mate, why not trust Him to also change your heart? Trust Him with your pain—your deep hurt—your grudge. Give Him the opportunity to remove your bitterness. Seek His intervention.

Far too often, we want the promises of the Lord without the conditions. We want the manifestations—we want prosperity, we want peace, we want power, we want deliverance—without its costing us anything. The Lord promises to manifest Himself to those who love Him, to those who both accept and obey His commands (see John 14:21). Loving, accepting, obeying—truly seeking the Lord—requires something from us. But it is amazing what delighting ourselves in the Lord daily will do to our lives. It may even change our heart. If you want to deal with the deep hurt—and believe it is beyond your power to control—take it to the Lord. But do so diligently. As David instructed:

> Commit thy way unto the Lord; trust also in him; and he
> shall bring it to pass.
>
> Psalm 37:5

You may find it helpful to recruit a confidant—one whose spirituality you have confidence in—to assist you. Accountability is good when dealing with the deep hurts. Go together before the Lord and ask for His healing. Holding on to a grudge can destroy your marriage. But it doesn't have to happen.

12

Extending Trust

The relationship could no longer be as it was. That was the decision made before dealing directly and constructively with the offending mate. Expectations, needs, what could and could not be lived with—all of these were expressed in a declaration that marked a turning point in the marriage. Either progress would be made toward the return of hope or reconciliation would probably always remain out of grasp.

Things began to change. There was first a coming to senses: an ownership of responsibility on the part of the mate, an admission of wrong. This confession was followed by genuine remorse for the pain suffered by the spouse. A change of heart was followed by a sincere commitment to the marriage and behavior that demonstrated a genuine change in the offender. All of these were wanted. All of these were needed. All of these were considered essential prerequisites to truly reconciling the marriage. But now, the spouse is hesitant. Why? Where is the problem? If things have progressed ideally to this point, why the hesitation?

Frequently, the hesitancy revolves around the issue of *trust*. Though the changes may be recognized, and the spouse would really like to feel confident and secure, a great deal of history continues to haunt the relationship. Resolving the issue of trust becomes the second major hurdle for reconciliation.

Trust is an emotional commodity. Though we may commit with our heads, we trust with our hearts. One is easier to control than the other. The real question becomes: Which will be allowed to control what is done?

Most of the Bible references on trust refer to our trusting in the Lord. But in his first letter to Timothy, the apostle Paul gives us some insight into trusting those whose past behavior may not necessarily warrant it. As we examine Paul's illustrations, we will find two themes: 1) trust *is not* extended lightly, and 2) trust *is* extended when warranted.

Trust *is not* extended lightly

In 1 Timothy, Paul expresses the theme that trust is not something to be extended lightly. True deliberation and evaluation are not only acceptable, but required. Paul is speaking to Timothy regarding church order and discipline. In an early chapter, Paul gives instruction regarding novices and those new to the faith. Seasoning, grounding, spiritual growth—Paul suggests that a time of proving oneself is a prerequisite to being placed in any position of responsibility. But in chapter five, he turns his attention to behavior, both appropriate and inappropriate. In verse 22 we gain some insight into dealing with an individual whose past behavior has been less than exemplary.

> Do not be over-hasty in laying on of hands in ordination
> (*or* in restoring an offender by the laying on of hands), or

> you may find yourself responsible for other people's
> misdeeds; keep your own hands clean.
>
> 1 Timothy 5:22

Paul was referring to an individual who had once been part of the church but for some reason had fallen away. Now he was returning. Was the offender forgiven? Absolutely. Was he accepted back into the fellowship? Surely. But was he placed back into a position of responsibility? Probably not. At least, not until he had had an opportunity to prove that he was truly a changed person and one who was ready for new responsibilities.

Paul suggests caution be the rule of thumb. "Do not be over-hasty. . . ." Let a little time go by. Watch for signs of legitimate change. Let the offender give some proof to his claims. And when change has been evidenced, the issue of further responsibility—or the issue of trust—can again be approached. Trust is not extended lightly.

Trust *is* extended when warranted

If there is a theme that rivals Paul's instruction to be cautious regarding the extending of trust, it is his own praise and thankfulness to Jesus Christ for His willingness to extend trust toward him. In chapter one of 1 Timothy, Paul again discusses behavior—both good and bad. He stresses how those who love the Lord will behave in one manner while those who do not will display behavior contradictory to "the gospel intrusted to me" (v. 11). What follows this differentiation of good and evil is not only a glimpse into Paul, but also a profound insight into the issue of trust.

> I thank him who has made me equal to the task, Christ
> Jesus our Lord; I thank him for judging me worthy of this

> trust and appointing me to his service—although in the past
> I had met him with abuse and persecution and outrage. But
> because I acted ignorantly in unbelief I was dealt with
> mercifully; the grace of our Lord was lavished upon me,
> with the faith and love which are ours in Christ Jesus.
>
> Here are words you may trust, words that merit full
> acceptance: "Christ Jesus came into the world to save
> sinners"; and among them I stand first. But I was mercifully
> dealt with . . .
>
> 1 Timothy 1:12-16a

I particularly like these final words—Paul's description of himself as a premier sinner—but in spite of this, Christ's merciful dealings. We can glean from this passage a model for extending trust. When do you extend trust? When it is warranted. When is it warranted? When there has been change. And how do you know whether there has been genuine change? You have to thoroughly evaluate the situation.

Paul professes to a past that was unacceptable:

> . . . I had met him with abuse and persecution and outrage.

But there was a change in Paul. And with the change came the opportunity for further evaluation.

> I thank him for judging me worthy . . .

Jesus is not prone to look lightly at anyone or anything. He is thorough in His assessments. Paul was no exception. But when he had been evaluated and found to be worthy, Paul praises his Lord for the next step in the sequence:

. . . judging me worthy of this *trust* and appointing me to his service . . .

The biblical principles are clear. Trust is not to be extended lightly—especially when past behavior abused the privilege. However, when genuine change has been evidenced and evaluated, we are to do as the Savior does. Others should echo the words of Paul: "But I was mercifully dealt with . . ." Trust is extended when warranted.

A Willingness to Risk

Whenever I deal with a relationship where hope has been lost, the question of trust becomes an issue. It seems that, regardless of the changes made—regardless of the admissions, remorse, and commitment—extending trust to someone who had not handled it well in the past is very difficult. It requires a spouse to take a chance. It requires a willingness to risk.

Steve and Mary Jean both appeared anxious at our first meeting. As it turned out, their relationship had been through so much turmoil without a counselor, they were both a little surprised that things finally got to the place where professional help was sought.

They described a marriage that had been drifting for years. Sometimes the process of drifting apart is subtle and out of view. But for both Steve and Mary Jean, the reality of their failing relationship was clear. Yet neither one of them knew what to do to halt the process—so it continued. Mary Jean tried to stay connected by asking Steve questions about his work and talking of their plans for a new house. But their conversations were mostly superficial. Mary Jean found herself investing more of her energy into the children while Steve spent most of his free time working on race cars with his friends.

Things took a turn for the worse when Steve started recording frequent, unexplained absences. He had excuses, but they began to sound suspicious. The explanations went from working on a car at a friend's house, to going to work early or getting home late. And there were large gaps of time unaccounted for on his days off. Mary Jean began to suspect that Steve might be seeing someone else.

Mary Jean finally confronted her husband with her suspicions but Steve only responded with denial: "How could you think such a thing." Nothing changed—there were still unexplained absences and Steve seemed to drift even further away from Mary Jean. Then the phone calls started. They were always anonymous, but the caller named a person, place, and meeting times. These times coincided with some of the gaps in Steve's unexplained schedule. Mary Jean again confronted Steve. This time, he became incensed. Angrily, he continued the denial.

Mary Jean didn't know what to do or who to believe. Tension was mounting at home. She watched Steve's every movement. He responded with accusations that she was crazy with jealousy. "You're going to drive me away. I can't live like a trapped animal." Things finally reached a crisis when Mary Jean found a motel receipt in Steve's glove compartment. With something tangible in hand, the charade ended. Steve finally admitted his guilt.

There was a period of time when things got pretty difficult for the marriage. The future of the marriage came into question. There was a brief separation. But Steve was more interested in remaining married to Mary Jean and keeping his family together than he was in pursuing this other relationship, so with the help of their pastor, a reconciliation occurred.

It had been two months since Steve and Mary Jean had resumed living together. During that time, Steve had been a model husband. He was attentive, reliable, and accountable. He was all that Mary Jean had hoped he would be. Given all that they had been through, and with all of the positive changes that had occurred, why were they now coming for counseling?

> I just don't trust him. I wish I did. But I can't get rid of the memory of what he did to me.
>
> It's not an issue of forgiveness. It hurt me—but if I know my heart, I believe I have forgiven Steve for what he did. But it doesn't make trusting him any easier.
>
> He lied to me once before. How do I know he won't do it again? And even though he says he's home for good, how do I know he won't change his mind and leave me for someone else? If he did it once, how do I know that he won't do it again?
>
> This feeling of mistrust continues to nag me. I can't seem to get over it. And I know my checking up on Steve is driving him crazy. But I just can't stop it.

Mary Jean hadn't driven Steve crazy. But Steve did admit to a growing frustration regarding the persistence of the problem.

> I don't know what else to say or do. I was wrong and I'm sorry. I'm doing everything within my power to make it up to Mary Jean. But I don't know what else I can do.

As I began to work with Steve and Mary Jean, I first let them know just how normal they were. Though Mary Jean still had some unanswered questions regarding the affair—legitimate questions that would continue to haunt the relationship until Steve gave her some answers—resolving these questions only helped clean up their reconciliation. It did not resolve the issue of trust.

I explained the common, dual problem revolving around the trust issue. For the offended spouse, the feeling of apprehension is expressed in the statement "I don't trust you." For the offender, the feeling of frustration is expressed in the statement "I need to be trusted." This dilemma blocks further efforts toward reconciliation. Though both mates play a role in resolving the trust issue, an initial step must be taken by the offended spouse.

A mate must demonstrate changes before trust is again warranted. But if a spouse expects to become absolutely comfortable with the mate before trust can be extended, that time will never come. The offending mate cannot do enough to totally *earn* back the trust. At some point, a spouse will have to accept what is offered at face value and take a chance. A risk will have to be taken.

When you take a risk, you place yourself in a vulnerable position— you set yourself up for possible hurt. That is the negative part of taking a risk. The positive aspect, however, is the potential for gain. When dealing with a marriage where hope has been lost, there is always risk involved. But if you are unwilling to take a risk, there will be no gain.

As the three of us began to work on the marriage, Mary Jean had to choose to trust Steve. She began to realize that, although trust was something that Steve could ruin, he could not totally earn it back— at least, not at this time in their relationship. For the time being, trust, as an issue, was given a secondary status. We chose to focus on other aspects in their relationship.

The rule of thumb is that if a couple is working on the restoration of the marriage properly, it will take one to two years before trust ceases to be a concern. That is what it took for Steve and Mary Jean. It is never instantaneous. And it is not without occasional disruptions. There were times when Mary Jean's level of trust seemed to regress. But even with three steps forward and two steps back, progress was made.

Steve's demonstration of commitment, coupled with the passage of time, gradually resolved the trust issue in their marriage. But it began with Mary Jean's decision to extend it. Not that it had been totally earned—but it was warranted, and she was willing to take a risk. This allowed hope to return to their marriage.

Final Thoughts

"But I was mercifully dealt with . . ." As Christians, these are words that we can all echo. We do not always receive what we deserve. For this we should be thankful. It is a testimony to the Lord's love and grace that we are frequently the recipients of mercy instead of justice.

When it comes to marriage, there are bound to be times when we find ourselves in paradoxical roles. Sometimes we stand in the need of mercy, while at other times, we are the ones doing the dispensing. I do not believe that trust easily returns to a marriage where hope has been lost—where the repetition of unacceptable behavior has marred the memory of a relationship. But even though the return of trust can be marked with difficulty, this does not change the fact that it can return. And if trust is allowed to return at all, it will be because a spouse chose to dispense mercy. An offended spouse will have to be willing to take a risk. With the risk will come the potential for restoration.

13

A Sow's Ear

The old adage, "You can't make a silk purse out of a sow's ear," aptly describes the third hurdle for reconciliation. The decision was made that things had to change. The marriage could no longer be as it was. And as a result of direct confrontation and constructive work by both mates, things did begin to change. But how much change is enough? What is legitimate to expect—and what is not? Maybe you don't need to settle for a sow's ear. But does that mean you can expect a silk purse?

This was the question that puzzled Mark and Kathy. They had been married long enough to have grandchildren. Though Kathy had been dissatisfied with her and Mark's relationship over much of their married life, the intensity of this dissatisfaction seemed to increase with age. Finally, she sought some professional help.

Kathy's central complaint was Mark's absence from the relationship. Though Mark had always been responsible, accountable, and stable, his presence in the marriage had been primarily in body only. He was absent emotionally, and it was this absence that frustrated Kathy the most.

Mark could easily be described as a classic emotional distancer. As such, he displayed some very common characteristics. He was most comfortable with superficial relationships. Therefore, a safe emotional distance was preferred over closeness. He had many acquaintances, but few true friends. And even with those who he indeed counted as friends, their connection was largely through hobbies and career. They had the traditional conversations: sports and work. Nothing got any deeper.

Most of an emotional distancer's energies are directed out of the marriage. Usually the career is a large recipient. But outside hobbies and interests can also be included. The successful career man is also gone a lot playing golf, or fishing, or following sporting activities, or . . . Mark was no exception. He had a lot of outside interests—things that for years had kept him moving away from Kathy, toward the outer fringes of his marriage.

Kathy had wanted more from the marriage than a view of Mark's back as he headed out the door. But years of chasing, pleading, and demanding had not changed anything. In fact, it probably only heightened their friction. Finally, Mark's emotional absence took its toll. In utter frustration, Kathy gave up. It was then that she came for counseling.

Eventually, Mark also came to counseling. But it was apparent that this was an appeasing maneuver on his part. His goal was not for personal change. Rather, it was to pacify Kathy. "How can I keep my marriage together without changing?" If he could just get Kathy calmed down, he could resume his old pattern. Things could go back to the way they were. Mark could continue to keep himself at a comfortable distance, and Kathy could resume her uncomfortable pursuit. But this was not to be. Kathy was no longer willing to play the old game. She would not be pacified. She would not be duped. She expected real change.

The first year that we worked together was crisis-prone and intense. Kathy and Mark would play particular roles during the counseling sessions. Kathy would be hurt, wounded, threatening, and angry; Mark would be confused: "I don't understand what you want from me." There was even a brief separation. Finally, we began to turn a corner in the relationship. Mark genuinely recognized his limitations and how these had interfered with the development of a stable marriage. With this realization, we were able to change the direction of counseling. Over the next six months, we began to focus more on healthy and appropriate behavior.

I began to stress the theme: "Invest in your marriage." As such, I cited three forms of marital investment: 1) cooperate with me, 2) deal with me, and 3) talk to me. *Cooperate with me* refers to the division of labor to run a home and how we spend our time. Who does what at home and how is that decided. Ideally, mates cooperate to make these decisions rather than responding selfishly. *Deal with me* refers to the degree mates deal with one another regarding dissatisfactions. Ideally, areas of dissatisfaction will be approached directly and honestly and not avoided. *Talk to me* refers to a mate's willingness to be self-disclosing. How open is a mate about what he thinks and what he feels? Is he sharing himself with his mate? In a healthy and growing marriage, investment is made in all of these areas.

In the three areas of investment, Mark had always been fairly cooperative. He hadn't invested much time into joint activities. But neither had he been selfish. He had always done his fair share of the work around the house, willingly performing the perfunctory tasks. As an emotional distancer, his greatest limitations were sharing and dealing with dissatisfactions. Kathy's greatest complaints, therefore, were always: "Mark won't deal with me" and "Mark won't talk to me."

Dealing and talking were the areas that had been receiving the greatest amount of attention during the last few months of counseling. "What stops you from dealing with Kathy? What stops you from allowing her to deal with you? Why are you uncomfortable with sharing? Where does that come from? How can that be changed?" This had been the focus of therapy and it seemed that progress was being made. Then, toward the end of a fairly intense session, Mark suddenly made an announcement: "I want a sabbatical."

The room grew quiet at Mark's statement. Kathy was visibly surprised. She was also confused. What did Mark mean by a sabbatical? And why did he want one now?

> I'm not quitting. I just want a break. I feel as though I've been working pretty hard at changing some things that have been in place for a lot of years. But I also feel as though I'm not getting much recognition for my efforts. I know I'm not getting any appreciation.
>
> I'm tired. I want a sabbatical. I want an opportunity to be who I am and not feel pressured because I'm not something else. After a rest, I'll probably be ready to resume working on things again. But for now, I want a break.

Mark was angry when he made his announcement. I don't know that a sabbatical was the best idea for their relationship. But I do think his feelings were legitimate.

Mark will always be limited when it comes to interpersonal relationships. He was doing better. And with time and effort, Mark could continue to demonstrate gradual improvement. But he will never be great. Seldom will a man like Mark go from poor to great. He can move from poor to better, and better may be sufficient. But it is highly unlikely that what he will be able to offer the relationship emotionally could ever be considered great. This was a reality that Kathy would have to accept—but she had not yet accepted it.

There is a fine line separating what is healthy and legitimate to expect and what is not. Sometimes the differentiation of the two is further complicated by the natural limitations of the mates involved. Mark's limitations serve as an example of just such a complication. Throughout most of their marriage, Mark had behaved as a sow's ear. He had offered little to the marriage. With help and intent, he could become an acceptable tote bag. But he would never become a silk purse. To cling to the expectation of a silk purse relationship, therefore, would not only result in frustration for Kathy, but for Mark as well.

I am not saying that Kathy's expectations were unreasonable. Her desires for a husband who would easily deal and talk were *ideally* legitimate. However, they were *practically* illegitimate after taking into consideration the man who was her husband. Kathy wanted and deserved more from Mark than she had experienced. And Mark was capable of giving more to the marriage than he had previously given. But adjustments would have to be made regarding expectations if the changes being made in this marriage were not to stall. There were definite limitations regarding what Mark could realistically offer.

Accepting Limitations

Resolving over-expectations is a hurdle which must be successfully cleared if a relationship is to move toward complete reconciliation. To aid this resolution, there are several factors to consider.

Differentiate between limitations and deviancy

Behavioral limitations may have some undesirable qualities. However, with appropriate modification, these limitations can prove to be acceptable. Deviant behavior, on the other hand, is never acceptable.

I once met with a client whose husband constantly accused her of being unloving because she refused to accept him as he was. He reasoned that, if she were the Christian woman that she claimed to be, she would accept him even though he differed from her expectations. And what was this difference that seemed to present the difficulty? What were his limitations? Simply this: he was a drug user. What he called a difference and limitation she called deviant. And she was correct.

When dealing with deviant behavior, we are not looking at gradations. Moving from poor to better will not suffice. Deviant behaviors are unacceptable. Their unacceptability is not based on their undesirability. Rather, they are unacceptable because they are wrong.

When evaluating the issue of realistic limitations, it is imperative that a behavior first be examined by this criteria. A behavior can be undesirable and not deviant. As in the situation with Mark and Kathy, failing to deal and talk was undesirable marital behavior. It greatly interfered with the development of a healthy and productive relationship. Though undesirable, however, these tendencies to avoid were not deviant in nature. There were possibilities for modification. Deviant behaviors, on the other hand, are both undesirable and unacceptable.

The very nature of deviant behavior is wrong. Whether the behavior is abusive or addictive, there is no room for mere modification. These are not limitations which need to be realistically accepted. They are problems which must be successfully faced and resolved by the offending mate. Anything short of this will only result in further heartache.

Do not take limitations personally

Part of what kept Mark and Kathy's relationship intense, even after Mark was making definitive efforts toward change, was Kathy's tendency to take Mark's limitations personally. Mark had difficulty sharing his feelings. But this was a generic problem. He rarely shared with anyone. It was not as if he shared his feelings with everyone except Kathy. No. He did not share at all. But Kathy had difficulty recognizing this fact.

To Kathy, Mark's failure to share was interpreted as a personal rejection. She placed a meaning on his behavior that was not intended. And by so doing, she further complicated an already difficult situation.

Sometimes, limitations are person-specific. For example, a mate may be willing to share with others but resists doing so with his spouse. If this is the case, then attention needs to be given to the specific problem in that relationship. Where is the blockage? What is stopping the mate from sharing? However, sharing is more likely to be a generic characteristic than it is to be specific to a mate. When this is the case, recognize the reality of the situation. Do not place more meaning and significance on the particular behavior than it warrants. Taking a mate's limitation personally only interferes with the ultimate goal of reconciliation.

Be willing to work with the limitation

When Paul and Glenda first came to my office, the decision to separate had been reached by Glenda and resisted by Paul. Showing up for counseling was Paul's attempt at changing Glenda's mind. Though agreeable to continued counseling, however, Glenda was intent on moving out. She had had enough of Paul's behavior and it would take more than his promise to go to counseling for her to stay home.

As we delved into the marital history, Glenda described a relationship which depicted her as a giver and Paul as a taker. He was reportedly selfish, domineering, and largely insensitive to her desires. Things went best if Glenda simply supported Paul's dreams and schemes. On those rare occasions when Glenda felt inclined to challenge Paul's position, the result was turmoil. Peace would return to the marriage only after she—and not Paul—would acquiesce.

After several minutes of unflattering description, accompanied by numerous examples, I expected Paul to refute in some way. To my surprise, Paul confirmed everything that Glenda had said. To my further surprise, he suggested that such behavior on his part was perfectly legitimate. After all, that was the way he had always been. And he was the head of the home. So, where was the problem?

Obviously, there was nothing said during that session to offer Glenda any hope for the future of the marriage. Neither was there anything said that would prevent her from moving out. I continued to counsel with them, but rather than seeing them together, chose instead to work with them individually.

Paul and I began to explore his natural, yet non-productive, behavior. We identified his selfish and manipulative lifestyle. We explored how it may have been developed—where the roots were. And we examined the relational consequences—how it interfered with the development of trust, respect, and emotional bonding. Gradually, Paul began to genuinely view his behavior as wrong. This was the real turning point in his marriage.

Interestingly, Paul's realization that selfishness and manipulation were wrong did not immediately change his behavior. These were deep patterns. Much time and effort would be required for significant change. But the corner had been turned. It was now imperative for Glenda to willingly work with Paul and his limitations. This is what Paul said to her.

> I've always been manipulative and selfish. This was true even when I was a little boy. I'm a natural salesman. But I don't want to be that way with you.
>
> I know I've taken advantage of you. And there will probably be times when I attempt that again. I know I can do better—and I want to. But I'm going to need your help to change.

Paul's desire to change was sincere. With this kind of commitment, Glenda was willing to take a chance. She began to point out both how and when Paul crossed her boundaries. Instead of retaliating or becoming overbearing, he would reflect and adapt. Slowly, their relationship began to change. Paul began to be less of a taker and more of a giver.

Their relationship is not ideal. Nor is it likely to ever reach that level. But within Paul's limitations, there has been some significant improvement. And with Glenda's help and acceptance of these limitations, progress should continue to be made.

Acknowledging behavioral limitations should not be taken as license

Sometimes a spouse is apprehensive about accepting any limitation at all, fearful that all accountability is then dismissed. "If you give him an inch, he will take a mile." No one is afraid to give up the inch. The anticipated relinquishment of the mile is frightening. What lengths does giving up the inch lead to?

If the attitude of the offending mate is truly to take the mile—to take the acknowledgment and acceptance of some degree of behavioral limitation as license—then the consequences for the relationship can be disastrous. But this may not be the mate's attitude.

This particular issue was a problem for Kathy and Mark. Kathy feared that, if she gave Mark any slack at all, he would quit trying altogether. And this thought—that Mark would quit trying to change— terrified her. Consequently, rather than being able to rest in the advances that were taking place, Kathy constantly pointed out Mark's deficiencies. This led to Mark's sabbatical.

Possible abuse which can come from the acceptance of limitations can be reduced by stating expectations clearly. Articulate what is acceptable and what is not. Acknowledge the mate's difficulties, while expressing appreciation for his efforts. Try to be both realistic and cooperative. But leave no doubt that there is still accountability.

The acceptance of limitations should never be construed as license to continue in unacceptable behavior. But neither should the fear of such a possibility hold back progress in the marriage. Demonstrated behavior, and not fear, should be the only indicator for a spouse's decision.

14

A Change of Hearts

Ed and Margie had the kind of relationship that therapists like to describe as "challenging." This is similar to a realtor's use of the phrase "a real handyman's special," an optimistic expression for a house that is in dire need of repair. Generally, you should not buy such a house unless you either own a home construction company or have a brother-in-law who is a contractor. Ed and Margie's marriage was a real handyman's special. It desperately needed some attention.

Speaking with either Ed or Margie apart from the other, you would never have guessed that they had spent nearly thirty years bickering and arguing. Each independently appeared cooperative, congenial, and pleasant. Ed was a successful businessman and an active layman in their church. He taught a Sunday school class and was a member of the church board. Margie was a homemaker, having raised three children. Their youngest had just entered college. Margie, like Ed, was active in their local church, devoting most of her energies to women's ministry programs and outreach Bible studies. Ed and Margie appeared to be an ideal couple—to be every pastor's dream. But their relationship was actually far from ideal, far from being a marriage made in heaven.

The battle lines for this couple were firmly entrenched. Margie accused Ed of being controlling, domineering, insensitive, and unreasonable. Ed countered with a description of Margie as being totally and absolutely resistant.

> If I say "black," Margie says "white." If I say "yes," Margie says "no." It makes no difference what the issue or problem may be. Her opposition is predictable. She intends to resist me any chance that she gets.

What brought Ed and Margie to me for counseling was an issue that they could not resolve. They could not arrive at a point of agreement. It was another example of Ed saying "yes" and Margie saying "no." Ed wanted to do something but he could not do it without Margie's consent—and she wasn't going to give it to him. She had resisted Ed's every effort to change her mind, so Ed decided they would try counseling.

Over the course of six sessions, we reasoned and re-reasoned their presenting issue time and time again. We got nowhere. I also heard several other examples illustrating the same pattern. As a matter of fact, I heard nearly thirty years' worth of examples. Ed would want to do one thing and Margie would take an opposing position. In the midst of one of our sessions, I formulated several questions:

> Is this a "marriageability" issue? Would either one of these people be suitable mates for anyone? Or is this a

"compatibility" issue? Is there something that just makes it difficult for Ed and Margie to get along with each other?

In an effort to clear up this confusion, I determined to find out exactly how and when this pattern of "control and resistance" began. We were able to trace the pattern as far back as their first year of marriage. Ed said he wasn't sure when it began. To the best of his recollection, Margie had always been difficult. But Margie had a better memory. She knew exactly when it began—and she knew why.

We had only been married for six months. Everything seemed fine up to that point. Ed was a little rigid and he definitely liked for things to go his way. But I was young, optimistic, and in love. With a little patience and giving on my part, Ed usually showed his more reasonable side.

Then there was that Friday in December—that infamous Friday. Ed got a call from his mother. She explained all the trouble she was having with Ed's younger brother. Ed's father had died two years earlier and this was the last child at home. But he seemed to be more than Ed's mother could handle. She wanted Ed and me to move back home and help her raise her son.

Ed hung up the telephone, turned to me and announced: "We're moving home." You could have knocked me over with a feather. What did he mean we were moving home? That wasn't just across town. Home was over two hundred miles away. And what about jobs? We had left home to establish ourselves in a better situation.

I was not a happy camper. But you know, it wasn't the moving home that really got to me. Granted, I didn't want to leave where I was, and I felt that there may have been some other alternatives, but I would probably have accepted the idea and adjusted to the move if Ed had just been willing to talk to me about it. But he wasn't.

Ed had made up his mind and that was all that mattered. As far as he was concerned, the issue was closed. We were moving. That's what really got to me—it was his total disregard for what I thought or how I felt. It was going to be "his" way or "no" way.

I decided right then and there, Ed may call the shots, but that doesn't mean I have to like it—and it doesn't mean I have to make it easy. Two can play at being stubborn.

Margie's memory shed a great deal of light on thirty years of bickering. Things began to make sense. I assessed that Ed and Margie were both marriageable. I even figured they could be compatible to one another. But for this to become reality, some definite changes on both of their parts would be required.

It would be overly simplistic to say that all that needed to be done was for Ed and Margie to go back and resolve that first issue— the beginning of the control-and-resistance cycle. That was probably the first real opportunity for Ed to display his need to exercise control. No, there would need to be a more basic change before this marriage would turn around.

Sure, both Ed and Margie were behaving poorly in this marriage. I felt it was Ed's controlling nature that set the tone. Margie was resistant, but this was more of a reactive maneuver on her part. In fact, it was somewhat self-protective. There was no telling what Ed might do if Margie offered no resistance at all. He would be free to do exactly as he pleased, with little regard for Margie's feelings. No, Ed would have to first recognize his error—his inappropriate behavior in this marriage—and then do something about it, before there would be hope for any true and lasting change.

Accepting responsibility for his wrongdoing was something that Ed was not willing to do. He had come to counseling hoping to get his way on a pressing issue. He had not come to get resistance. Ed said that he got enough of that at home. When I began to confront Ed with the facts of his marriage, he and Margie dropped out of counseling.

Margie kept in touch with me by making periodic telephone calls. These were usually of a crisis nature. Things progressively worsened as Ed demonstrated his willingness to go to severe extremes in order to get his way. With each step of escalation, Margie would call to either complain or to seek advice. First Ed cut off Margie's money by closing all of their joint checking accounts and reopening them in his name only. Then he took away her transportation. Ed even moved out of the house threatening to leave Margie penniless. With no money, and no way to get a job, Margie could not even hire an attorney to protect her rights. Things were deteriorating rapidly.

I hadn't heard from Margie for nearly a year. From the sound of our last conversation, I assumed the worse—that she and Ed, after thirty years of fighting, finally ended their marriage. You can well imagine my surprise when I found that they had scheduled an appointment to meet with me for another session. What was of an even greater surprise was the content of the session.

> Ed and I were talking about all that has happened during the past year—all the changes—and your name came up. We decided to come in and share the good news. You probably don't get that kind of feedback in most of your sessions. I know you didn't from us when we were here before.

Margie went on to explain, and Ed confirmed, that they had genuinely reconciled their relationship. Things had gotten to a low point as of my last conversation with Margie. She saw no hope in their marriage surviving. With its history, she wondered why it should. Then, out of the blue, Ed came home and said he wanted to start over.

> Ed came in and said he was sorry. I had never heard him say that in nearly thirty years of marriage. He said it was long overdue. Ed said he was wrong for treating me the way that he had for all these years and that, if I would give him a chance, he would make it up to me.
>
> I was stunned. In fact, I didn't say anything for a few moments. Ed said he could understand my being upset with him—he had done some pretty rotten things. But he hoped I'd forgive him or at least give him an opportunity to prove himself.
>
> Well, that's all I needed to hear. **That's all I *ever* needed to hear.** All of my resentment disappeared. It just melted away. I no longer needed to resist him. It's been so wonderful since that day. We're so happy.

Ed shared with me later that it was a friend of his, restating the facts that I had already told him, that finally broke through his denial. When he recognized how inappropriate he had behaved as a husband—when he finally came to his senses—the pain of all that he had put Margie through was almost unbearable. He was overwhelmed with remorse. Even if she were to totally reject him, he had to ask her forgiveness.

What a blessing. What a healing. There is nothing more exciting than to witness reconciliation—the healing of a relationship. But what really impressed me as I shared the joy of this couple was the realization that there had not been a change of heart in this marriage. **There had been a change of *hearts*.** True, Ed had experienced a genuine change of heart. He had come to himself; he had felt the pain of remorse; he had changed his behavior; and he had recommitted himself to Margie and their marriage. But more than that, the genuine change that was evidenced in Ed's life allowed hope to return for Margie. This change in Ed—this change of heart—prompted a change of heart for Margie as well. There was a change for both of them. There was a change of hearts.

The recurring theme throughout this book has been: **When mates have a change of heart, God's power for restoration and healing is revealed.** I firmly believe this. Hope is *lost* through the repeated inappropriate behavior of a mate. Hope is *restored* through the genuine change of the same behavior. This change is evidenced through the process of reconciliation.

There is a plan. There is a process whereby the Lord can lead a couple to healing. It is called reconciliation. The power of the Lord for healing is available to those who seek it, but only to the extent to which each is willing to live by His principles and to place himself under the Lord's control. **The possibility for the return of hope to a marriage is found *within* the Lord's plan for reconciliation.** As we commit ourselves to working through His process, we achieve His healing. This is what was experienced by Ed and Margie. This can be your experience as well. God is faithful.